Success,
Happiness & Manifesto
of
"HAPPISM"

Success,
Happiness & Manifesto
of
"HAPPISM"

DR. M. M. MOHARIR

TATE PUBLISHING
AND ENTERPRISES, LLC

Published by Tate Publishing & Enterprises, LLC
127 E. Trade Center Terrace | Mustang, Oklahoma 73064 USA
1.888.361.9473 | www.tatepublishing.com

Tate Publishing is committed to excellence in the publishing industry. The company reflects the philosophy established by the founders, based on Psalm 68:11,
"The Lord gave the word and great was the company of those who published it."

Book design copyright © 2013 by Tate Publishing, LLC. All rights reserved.
Cover design by Jan Sunday Quilaquil
Interior design by Gram Telen

Published in the United States of America

ISBN: 978-1-62854-895-2
1. Self-Help / Personal Growth / Success
2. Self-Help / Personal Growth / Happiness
15.09.01

DEDICATION

Dedicated to my parents who toiled lifelong to plant
good-deed-fruit-trees for my happiness.

Contents

Abstract

This thought provoking book is a practical guide for those who care about *personal success* and *happiness* in life. It also postulates a new World Order through the theory of *Happism*, aiming at permanent and sustainable happiness on Planet Earth. It reevaluates the Gross National Happiness (GNH) index, a measure of happiness in a nation. A new index called Gross National Success (GNS) is introduced to measure a success of any regime during its rule, for example, success of a given president of a country in his/her four years tenure.

Above discourse on *success* and *happiness* smoothly and naturally leads to the theory of *Happism*. This is a practically implementable theory to bring eternal peace and happiness to the world nations. It is a recipe to create heaven on Earth.

Furthermore, this *Happism* Theory alone can solve any national or international problem using a single System Oriented Solution (SOS) format based on a 360 degree, bias-free rationale derived from the Manifesto of *Happism* and its supporting principles. This SOS format is used here to obtain a concise solution of each of the following current world problems:

1. Civil War in Syria,
2. Gun Homicide Rate in USA,
3. Global Warming,

4. Palestine Problem,
5. Taliban and al-Qaeda in Afghanistan,
6. Problems in India,
7. Illegal Immigration in U.S.A. from USA–Mexico Border.

—DR. M. M. MOHARIR

November 26, 2012
9668 Babauta Road
San Diego, CA 92129
Email: drmmmoharir@gmail.com

Part 1
About Success and Happiness

Every human being in his/her lifetime directly or indirectly strives for success and happiness. It is essential to have a full understanding and comprehension of the connotations and hidden meanings behind these terms. Is it possible to define them uniquely and completely or are they totally subjective? In the chaos of answering this question, it reminds me of one philosophical principle: It is possible to formulate a fundamental law of nature governing an apparently chaotic phenomenon in the universe. Yes, we can fully understand what success is and what happiness in life is. To know these terms, we have to think about: Are these two the separate media or one single continuum that is the success-happiness continuum, just as what Einstein has defined as space-time continuum, and not space and time—two separate media?

What is success? Is this term subjective or objective? Is success essential to be happy in life or can one be happy without striving for success? The "Yes" answer to the latter will automatically tell us that happiness is a stand-alone medium and does not need success. Thus, the success-happiness continuum will then be converted into a single happiness medium propelling one to possible sublime bliss. The "No" answer implies that success-happiness continuum is one medium. Then one has to answer: Can success always lead to happiness or in other words can failure always lead to unhappiness?

Answers to all these questions and many more are extremely important to define the achievement in a stride for success and happiness in life.

Datum Level to Measure Success

Success in life is measured with respect to a certain datum level, the level defined by the heritage of a person. It is also sometimes defined by the luck factor. The luck factor is governed by the forces from the fifth dimension, the forces beyond any subject's control. We will speak about them later. Let us talk about the heritage factor which defines the level of accomplishment or success in life. When we think about it, it is obvious for us that success is not an absolute term. It is relative to the datum level of heritage. By heritage I mean: The circumstances in which one is born and brought up. Obviously, the success of a president's son becoming a president and success of an average person's son becoming a president are two different levels of achievement in life. Unfortunately, I have observed many people at high level (that is people born with silver spoons in their mouths), forget this obvious difference because they forget the concept of datum level.

One may come across a family in which the father is a very successful entrepreneur, owner of a huge house with swimming pool, tennis court, well-maintained rose garden, etc. His children may be heard boasting that all of them got business degrees from a prestigious school in the country. What the siblings forget that if they were born in an average income family they might not have received the admissions in that prestigious school. There are hundreds and thousands like them with the same or better SAT scores, etc., which are the true measures of success of any individual student. The father's success in the business made the difference. Of course, I give credit to the boasting siblings for not getting spoiled in spite of the wealthy environment. However, when they boast, they forget that they have yet to prove the validity of their boasting. I understand that boasting cannot be valid at any time, but, at the same time, it should not be an empty boast.

Success, Luck, and Happiness

When one forgets that success is measured from an individual datum, one may tend to be unduly unhappy in life. It may lead to the envy and malice towards those who are at higher positions because of their highly elevated datum. In an ideal case, happiness is not adversely influenced by a failure when one thinks about it calmly. A person successful in his endeavor and one who has failed in it can both be happy in life. One has to understand that success in life needs efforts, means, tenacity, concentration power, and finally luck (the beneficial forces from the fifth dimension, the forces beyond our control). If one has done all the first four factors to one's satisfaction and then the fifth factor, i.e. luck ruins the success, then one has nothing to regret. One can be at ease and happy in ones failure also, though the individual would have been happier if the favorable luck would have given him his desired success.

One may see a situation in life such as a valedictorian going to the last chance of SAT exam and gets into an accident, wasting his whole year of schooling. It needs wisdom to understand and digest the effect of forces from the fifth dimension. Without that one may get into the situation of being unduly unhappy. Thus, luck can affect success, but luck and failure should not adversely affect happiness.

Happiness without Struggle for Success

Life is too short to think all the time about success. I have seen a few wise people who understand this at a very early stage of life. They are happy and contented without striving for any success. The problem with this situation is that one should maintain the level of that wisdom for the rest of one's life. Otherwise, one may start envying those who are successful in life because of their continuous efforts. The person, who was happy initially without any efforts for success, may become unhappy and that too at a time when he cannot improve his lot due to time-constrained circumstances. I have seen so many such persons who think they are happy without any further efforts. But when they see a very successful person, who has achieved success through one's own continuous efforts, they start pitying themselves and feel miserable. To be happy in life without being successful needs real wisdom, wisdom that will not fail you even in the later part of your life.

One can come across a few holy personalities who have no material possessions. In fact, they have never hankered after material success. Some of them are learned and some of them are uneducated, but they are happy and contented in life. They are true wise people. They observe the struggles of a common man. The source of their happiness is the inner thought that they are free from such struggles. To be happy, they will not create trouble for others. In fact, some of them may try to solve the problems of a common man. These are the wise sages. Some of them are born wise, and some achieve wisdom through early experiences in life. But they are the ones who achieve total eternal bliss. How many of such wise people that one sees in life?—I guess very few.

Ordinary or Extraordinary Success

The most important thing in life is to understand at every stage what you want out of life, and also, to be consistent about your expectations from life. Rolling Stones are generally miserable unless their successive wants or expectations are complimentary to the previous one. Serious change in midcourse correction may result in inner conflicts and pains. The question is: How many of us really know what we want out of life at a very early age?—And also how many of us are consistent with it throughout one's life span? Now, consider a general situation of a common man when he strives for that instant success, which gives him instant gratification. The key to temporal success is sincerity of purpose and hard work with deep concentration.

Such momentary success can be a useful stepping stone for his overall success in life. He may not realize it at that instance. But when he looks back in life, he may understand the importance of it. Eventually, for the common man, the chain of temporal successes may ultimately define his overall success. But, this is for a common man. Extraordinary people have one consistent aim in life. Many of them achieve it at a very early age; thus, eliminating the need of small stepping stones of the later part of life. Good examples are the scientists like Einstein, Newton, Heisenberg, etc. What enabled these people to achieve such extraordinary recognition at such an early age? Is it heritage/nurture/virtues/ destiny or something else?

Virtue: A Link between Success and Happiness

Let us see what role virtues play in achieving success and happiness? To be successful in life, one need not be virtuous. But to be happy, one must have success through virtues. Virtues are the force-carrying particles which link success to happiness. We see many Mafia people rolling in wealth. So, through a common man's perspective, they may be successful, but they may always be worried about their Mafia empire, about the encounter with the law, etc.

In this context some people, including myself, believe the philosophy presented in the story of "The Nectar Pot." A man owns a pot. A good amount of nectar is added to it whenever he does a righteous deed.

He can happily enjoy that nectar every day. But when he acts sinfully a hammer automatically comes and strikes that pot. A stage comes in his life when the pot cannot sustain any more impact and breaks down with the next instance of his sinful act. The nectar is spilled and the man is permanently unhappy.

Success achieved through virtues is a real source of happiness. A good test of a happy person is when he is alone, thinking about his past, present, and future; has a big smile on his face; and he is internally very contented. The point is, one can be a fake in the presence of others, but, when one is all alone, one cannot cheat one's inner voice and thoughts. One's facial expressions and inner thoughts are the true mirrors about the state of one's happiness or unhappiness. When one achieves success by hidden bad means, one will fake it in the presence of a company and show one's virtuous side only. But when one is alone, one cannot cheat oneself. All the crooked reasoning and rationale one comes up with in presence of others, collapse like a sand castle when one is all alone. Thus, success without virtues is not a real success. An exception to this principle is the success bestowed on you through luck.

"Some are born great, some achieve greatness, and some have greatness thrust upon them," English poet and playwright William Shakespeare has once said.

A person winning millions of dollars through lottery can be materially successful as well as very happy through material comforts. But will he be internally happy?—Why not—If he has not done any harm to anybody nor has any ill-feelings for the fellow beings! But such are very exceptional situations.

Shakespeare and the Story of the Four Fish

When Shakespeare wrote, "Some have greatness thrust upon them," what was in his mind? We do not know exactly. But such forced greatness can be through heritage or through forces from the fifth dimension. The example of greatness through heritage is often seen in political dynasties. A person may not be capable but will be a president or a prime minister of a nation. There comes the concept of datum level as a measure of success. A common man should understand that such a person is not successful simply because he is a president or a prime minister. Invariably such a person is asked to accept that position by his political cronies; thus thrusting so called greatness upon the person, the way Shakespeare has mentioned.

"Some are born great"—what is the connotation or hidden meaning behind this phrase? My understanding is: Such people through their body chemistry or genes or their god-given brilliance are destined to be great. This reminds me of a story of a boy and his four fish. The boy had a fish tank with four different types of fish. The boy would feed the fish by collecting the worms from the nearby stream. Sometimes, these worms were harmful to the fish because of the upstream pollution in the stream. When the boy fed harmful worms, the Type 4 fish did not know that the worms were no good. It would eat those worms and get sick. This happened continuously, bad worms were fed and the Type 4 fish got sick. The Type 3 fish, initially, did not know how to distinguish between a good and a bad worm. But after eating bad worms a couple of times, it could differentiate between them and would not eat them; thus, avoiding sickness. The Type 2 fish was a little smarter. Instead of eating the worms immediately, it would observe the other fish, and if they got sick, it would not eat that batch of worms. The Type 1 fish from the very beginning by its intrinsic quality could distinguish good worms from the bad ones.

When Shakespeare wrote, "Some are born great", he meant like those Type 1 fish in the story. To tell you the truth, I have seen very few personalities that are "born great". Mostly luck/personal efforts/heritage/ circumstances/ and/or their relative combinations, the way I see it, have made great people great. The exceptions I can think of are prodigies such as Beethoven, Mozart, Botvinnik, etc. But they are so rare. In actual practice, we also see some small kids having exceptional memories to remember long and difficult poetry (such as Sanskrit script of *The Geeta*), one can play some instrument at a very early age, etc. But those kids fade away in the later parts of life. A "born great" person has those exceptional qualities from his/her birth and continues to shine throughout his/her life. In this context we should understand the difference between a prodigy and a genius. A prodigy is born with a certain quality which may or may not last lifelong. Geniuses are those who "achieve greatness". Of course, some of those, who achieve greatness, may not be geniuses.

Einstein: Born Great or Achieved Greatness?

A case in study is physicist Albert Einstein. It is needless to say that Einstein was a super genius. His General Theory of Relativity also known as the Gravitational Field Theory is perhaps the most brilliant innovation of a human brain in the history of the human race (Only parallel, maybe, to the genius of physicist Isaac Newton). It is also believed that if Einstein was not born, this theory would not have been discovered for the next one hundred years. Given this situation I will say, Einstein "Achieved greatness." To achieve such tremendous success, personal efforts, concentration power, sincerity of purpose, and nurtures during his childhood and boyhood played significant roles.

Is there something like a "God-given brainpower"? How many people do we see in actual life like that Type 1 fish? How many Beethovens, Mozarts, and Botvinniks have we seen in our lives? Heritage, childhood and boyhood nurtures, and the environment into which one is born and brought up may not be necessary or sufficient conditions to achieve success in life, but they can act as a GPS (Global Positioning System) system guiding one to the proper path toward a successful life. Think about Einstein's upbringing during his childhood and boyhood: his early defect in speech made him an introvert leading him to his gedankenexperiment technique; his encounter with the magnetic compass gave him the idea of "Field Theory" leading to the Gravitational Field Theory i.e., the General Theory of Relatively; his uncle giving him a book of *Algebra* when he was about ten years old, whet his appetite for mathematics; his readings of all those mathematics and physics books from the age of twelve to fourteen, given by Max Talmey who also supplied him original philosophical books by Kant, Hegel, Mach, etc., leading him to the idea of the Relatively Theory, etc. Such type of upbringing can play an important role toward the success in the later part of person's life.

Gravity Waves and the Wiring of the Brain

In practice, we see different siblings achieving different degrees of success even though they went through the same upbringing; why is this so? My opinion is that the parents may give the same environment to each sibling, but they cannot control his/her thinking process. Outside influence, other than of the parents, may be different from sibling to sibling. God-given health or health at the time of birth may be different from person to person. Also, the planetary position at the time of birth varies from person to person. This last sentence may open a can of worms. But let me write down my thoughts on this subject: Astrology related to horoscope is an empirical science based on a statistical data accumulated for many centuries. I have seen some genuine astrologers, who have never seen you in your entire life, telling your past so accurately that you do not want to hear your future because of the fear of knowing something bad occurring in your future. I have seen and experienced myself how accurately these genuine astrologers can predict the future. The original question is: what has the planetary position at the time of birth do with that individual's future? We know horoscope is based on the place of birth (latitude and longitude) and the planetary position at the time of birth.

Planets are continuously bombarding the Earth with their respective gravity waves. These waves are some sort of radiation. When a fetus is in the womb of a mother, surrounded by the seminal fluid, these waves may not reach the brain of the fetus. The brain is then basically a blank uninitialized CD. At the time of birth when the brain is exposed to these gravity waves from various planets, the brain's circuitry is wired first time, or so to say, initialized. This initial wiring of the brain is crucial for the future behavior and feelings of that individual. Intensity and angle of incidence of a gravity wave from a planet depend on the position of the planet related to the place of birth on Earth. Therefore, timing and location (latitude, longitude) of birth is so important in generating a horoscope.

In the light of this discussion it is obvious that even though the parents may give the same environment to all the siblings, the latter may have a different degree of success in life. The external influence, other than of the parents, may differ from sibling to sibling as we discussed earlier. The bottom line is the horoscope along with the childhood and boyhood nurtures can play a crucial role in the future success of an individual. Einstein, without some of his upbringing episodes, would not be the Einstein we know today. We will see ahead that appropriate wiring of brain circuitry depicted in horoscope, which also represents destiny factor, is a necessary but not a sufficient condition to achieve Einstein type greatness.

Destiny and Datum Level of Happiness

Now, what is the reason that some of the people totally deprived of any comfortable childhood with junkie or very ordinary parents do achieve spectacular success in life? The answer is hidden in the above two paragraphs. The answer is destiny; the brain is wired such that all their actions and emotions goad them to do extraordinary things. I believe in destiny. Your destiny is written in your horoscope. When people say that you can alter the course of destiny, I know that such people are ignorant of the connotation behind the word destiny. Destiny is the one which totally controls all your actions and emotions at every stage of your life. This is the reason, two brothers of different ages with exactly the same family and social environment of upbringing end-up living different lives—one becomes a millionaire and the other remains a pauper. This does not mean that you should not put up any efforts in life and leave everything to destiny. By definition, what you do and think is your destiny. Destiny is written in your horoscope and accordingly you act and think.

This discussion creates a funny situation. Two kids, one boy and one girl, born exactly at the same time at the same place (same latitude and longitude), the boy's parents are very rich and the girl's are somewhat poor. The comforts these two will experience in life will be very different. This leads us to another important concept about happiness. Happiness also has Datum Level from where the former can be measured. Even though, the boy gets a dress of say $500 and the girl gets the one of $50, their levels of happiness will be the same, since these levels are measured from different datum.

Continuing the above example of the rich boy and the poor girl, consider this. Since their horoscope is exactly the same, certain planetary position may say that they both will get excellent jobs. The rich boy will get a job of say $200,000 per year, whereas the poor girl gets of $50,000 only. But for both of them their respective jobs are excellent, as predicted by the horoscope. Their levels of success and happiness are exactly the same. Obviously, this is because they are measured from different datum levels.

Why so much discussion about destiny, horoscope and the astrology?—It gives us different perspectives on success and happiness in life. Even though, one may not believe in astrology, the conclusions based on it are true for all the circumstances.

Wealth, Wisdom, and Happiness

Life is unpredictable for those, who cannot plan properly, (barring the situation of the forces from the fifth dimension, the luck factor). Unhappy are those who deserve to be unhappy, again, barring the extreme bad luck factor. Virtues and wisdom play major roles in making a man happy or unhappy. External environment has nothing to do with it. One can see so many poor people enjoying life. They are wise and virtuous because they know their own limitations, particularly those imposed by the surroundings, and they are not envious of the rich people. Of course, it takes a special breed of poor people to achieve this state of happiness. I do not mean to say here that the poor people should think wisely, be virtuous, and stay in their poor environment their whole lives. What I mean to say is: Unhappy are those who deserve to be unhappy barring the extreme bad luck factor.

The same principle is applicable to the rich, also to all in between the rich and the poor. In short, we have drifted to the question, what has wealth got to do with happiness? The answer is simple; happiness is tied with wisdom and virtues and not with the wealth. A rich man, always greedy, may not sleep happily at night. Another rich man who has done a lot of good things for the society, and acquired his wealth through his virtues and not by means of vices, can be very happy.

Time Dependent Success and Happiness

The urge of success and happiness is time dependent. In old age, success is a past entity whereas urge or desire of happiness is for the present and the future. An old person can be happy in his old age while looking back at his past success, but very rarely, will he strive for a current or future success. This situation is just reversed during the young age. A young man desires present success at any cost. He is ready to sacrifice his comforts, such as his sleeping hours, to achieve current success. That does not mean that the young man is unhappy. He may consider it his duty to work hard and improve the lot for himself and his family. Moreover, his life is full of hope for future and comfortable living. That hope is a source of his happiness. Consider a case of a successful student. He studies when others are partying. But his source of happiness is his past academic achievements and his hope of guaranteed excellent success in future examinations. The subtle point is, the current success is the young man's aim. He will feel happy about it in the future. For an old man, his current aim is happiness. He has no desire left to aim for any more success in life.

The fulfillment of personal desire for success through the achievement of one's children is a common practice among the failures or lazy people. Success cannot be transferred like this from person to person. The father who has failed to achieve his own desired success may feel happy that his son is successful. But this happiness cannot substitute the happiness the father would have derived, if he himself would have succeeded in reaching his own goal. Such failed father may be unduly harsh and disciplinarian towards his kids just to fulfill his own ambition which he could not do so because of his own laziness or mistakes in his past. But if this failed father has failed not because of his own shortcomings but because of the forces from fifth dimension, then it can be a different situation. The father by his own experience can anticipate such forces and nullify their effects from the life of the son. (Note here that forces from the fifth dimension cannot be avoided, by definition. But the impact of their effects can be softened.) This helps the son to achieve the desired goal in life. In this situation, the achievement of the son will give the father the same happiness as if the father himself has achieved his own desired goal, which he could not achieve in the past because of the forces from the fifth dimension.

Deriving the old age happiness through the success of one's own kids is natural to human beings. Nothing is wrong with that, but using it as a substitute for one's failed efforts and ambitions can result in a family conflict. The son's ambition may not be the same as that of the father. The son's aptitude can be different. The best way is to leave the son alone striving for the success, defined by his own aptitude. The efforts of the father come into picture only when the son is walking on a wrong path. The father unduly interfering in the efforts of the son to reach the self-defined well-intentioned destination can result in total chaos, complicating or even ruining the life of the son. Most of the time, the father's unfulfilled aim has nothing to do with the life ambition of the son.

Hidden Source of Ambition

The urge for a successful life differs from person to person. The origin of such an urge is so varied. Many people believe in a doctrine: Never go in a company where you are neither respected nor loved. I do not believe in it. You may go in such a company, understand each individual character therein, and expect actions and words from that character accordingly. The major source of disappointment is false expectation. Disappointment can cause unhappiness. But on the other hand, the above situation is a good source of the urge for more and more successes in life. You may work hard with a cool brain for your temporal successes one after another, which may eventually define the total success in your life. While you are trapped in a company where you are neither respected nor loved, there will be some cunning persons who will try to show that they are your friends, but in their hearts they are your ill-wishers. They wish that you should fail in your endeavor, but they may not have any influence on the outcome of your efforts. Such ill-wishers very subtly show their bad inner feelings towards you, when you are in their company. If you are smart with a cool brain, you'll understand their envious feelings toward you. Believe it or not, this will be your source of urge for a bigger and a better success in life. It is sort of a cat-and-mouse game you play with these bad guys. The more subtle and hidden bad feelings they expose toward you, the more you enjoy the successive successful stages in your efforts toward the final temporal success.

If this cat-and-mouse game causes distraction in your efforts towards your desired success, then better avoid these ill-wishers and be free to think and act coolly towards your aim. If you cannot withstand the heat of the kitchen, then you better leave it.

Lonely at the Top

No doubt, your success breeds more enemies against you, just as the one in the above discussion. No one says: success can always bring happiness. The word "always" is important here. Apart from the hard work demanded to be successful, the success itself has some germs of unhappiness. You may leave behind your near and dear ones. The childhood friends, who were ready to do anything for you, may show aloofness toward you even though your success has not changed your childhood affection towards them. Your own family members may create family problems for you. The sibling rivalry may be on the rise, etc. The successful man should treat all these situations as a resultant of the forces from the fifth dimension. In this situation your wise actions and words give very fruitful results since you are dealing with those who are so near and dear to you. Also, they had considered you to be one of them. This situation is just a hundred and eighty degrees opposite to the one of the company which does not love or respect you.

It is also said, "It is lonely at the top." This is true. When you reach the top (measured from the individual datum), what you may have with you is your own sense of achievement. You may be happy or unhappy based on the mixture of vices and virtues you have employed while reaching the top. One may think that one does not have to be lonely at the top because one can have the company of the people who have reached their respective tops. But believe me, it is not the same as having the company of your near and dear ones. The company of the tops is just a time-pass. What is there with you is your sense of achievement and your state of happiness or unhappiness depending on your vices and virtues.

Past Laurels

In this discussion one should remember what Edmond Hillary has said. Edmond and Sherpa Tensing were the first human beings to climb Mt. Everest. They did so in the year 1953. One day some time in the nineteen seventies or so, Edmond was sitting alone in a lounge of a hotel in New Delhi. One newspaper reporter spotted him and asked, "Edmond, it is really an irony of the situation that no one even recognizes you now. Do you feel bad about it?" Edmond gave a nice answer to that reporter, "No, I do not feel bad about it because you cannot rely on the laurel achieved a few years back." The moral of the story is very clear. If we forget it, then there is a possibility of a gap existing between your expectation of respect and the one you receive from others. Such a gap can make you unhappy. After climbing your first peak of success, you may try another and then another, till you get old and then rely on so many laurels you have achieved throughout your life. That is the source of happiness in your old age. And of course, the level of happiness depends on the level of virtues employed during the conquest of these various peaks.

Exception to above discussion is the situation of an exceptional achiever. His achievement is so exceptional that he does not have to climb any new peak after the first big one. It is just a frosting on the cake, if he keeps on achieving more and more which may be or may not be as spectacular as the original success. Again, the case in point is of Einstein. His General Theory of Relativity was enough for him to rely on this laurel for the rest of his life.

Know Thyself

Now the question comes: How long should one keep on climbing such peaks of consecutive successes? The answer comes from philosophy: *Know thyself.* One may feel happy and contented after climbing a few peaks only. Others may keep on doing so till they are old—when physical limits constrain one's efforts. When I used to hear this philosophical phrase *Know thyself*, I would get confused and sometimes laugh at the sages using it in their sermons. At an occasion, I would get mad at these sages, falsely considering them to be hypocrites and con artists cheating the naive common public. There may be some cheaters like this, but the glass is half full or half empty. The person may be a cheater but the philosophy is pure gold.

Some say: Life is that as you take it. For me: Life is that as you make it. Every success is in your capacity, provided you understand the principle of Datum Level. Also, one has to remember that there is always a place at the top in any field. Individual smartness is to select an appropriate field with a path of least resistance. Undue efforts toward the area of unknown, or the path over which you are forcefully dragging yourself, may not lead to success but to disappointment and inferiority complex. There comes the philosophy of *Know thyself.*

Self-Enlightenment and Eternal Bliss

Many times, my friend and I discuss what made some individuals follow a particular route and become so successful. The answer is very complicated and hidden in all the pages given above. On the other hand, it is easy to answer how some people attain sainthood and the subsequent eternal bliss—the happiness all the time in all the circumstances. One highway to eternal bliss can be meditation. Here the term "meditation" is used with the connotation of "Self-enlightenment through inner thinking process, similar to what the Buddha practiced to acquire his wisdom."

Meditation does not need any external efforts. It is an internal struggle to conquer your worldly desires and fully control your thinking process. When you do not need any external efforts, there is no complication in what direction the efforts should be channeled. Of course, there is another path to happiness derived from the achievement of success. But this path is neither necessary nor a sufficient condition toward happiness. Whereas meditation itself can be enough to make one happy if one is wise and virtuous. These are the examples of sages and saints. Is it not a fact that many sages apparently do nothing? But they achieve their wisdom through their inertness which we may call as meditation. One can be happy through meditation, provided one can channelize one's thoughts in virtuous rational direction and one's feelings in a balance mode, as explained ahead in a story of "Line of Sight". Meditation can cool down your overheated brain; and also slow down your high gear, and out-of-control emotions.

Meditation clearly tells us that happiness is within you, it is an internal and not external entity. The life of a saint or sage may sometimes go through a difficult path physically but never mentally or emotionally. These people are cool; they do not have to worry for their families because they do not have the families to start with. Or better to say, the whole society or the whole world, (depending on the fame of the saint), is their family. If sainthood is such a bliss, then why is everyone not a saint? Obviously, the required condition to be a saint, i.e. one should be unmarried, is not so easy to fulfill. This again opens the can of worms. Does it mean that married people cannot be saints? My answer is: "Yes, married people cannot be saints." They may be saint-like but they are not saints. For example: a medical doctor, married but devoting his whole life toward curing the poor without expectation of any remuneration. I have been seeing such doctors since my childhood. They always received utmost respect from me. They are like saints to me. Secondly, there may be some married social workers whose actions and words are saint-like. They work without any propaganda of their work and as such hidden in the society. The point here is: there is a difference between a saint and a saint-like person, as explained in the next paragraph.

Is this happiness of a saint worth pursuing? First of all, this idea of sainthood should come at an early age before one gets married. Once you are married and then leave your family, or drag your family in poverty, to pursue sainthood, are your actions not desired through a moral obligation point of view? Such an injustice to your family will prevent you to attain sainthood and the subsequent eternal bliss. This idea of pursuing sainthood before marriage is hard to follow because that age is full of worldly desires. Those who follow true sainthood through virtues at an early age before marriage by means of meditation and self-study can reach sublime bliss and happiness. No sorrow can perturb their blissful state of mind. Such people I have seen are destined to be so through their horoscopes and planetary positions. Their family circumstance during childhood, or so to say their upbringing, has very little to do in selecting the path towards their sainthood. They are of fish Type 1 personality. This should answer the question: if one should strive for happiness through sainthood. In the post-married life you may try to follow the path of sainthood by helping others without any expectation in return. That will define you as a good man not as a saint. Eternal bliss of a saint is very different.

Religion: Path to Happiness or Destruction

Life is full of selfish people. What percentage of them is made up of crooks, cheaters, and, in general, bad guys, depends on the characteristics of the society. We say: all the religions aim at making the followers virtuous, but the problem comes in interpreting the religious scripts.

This interpretation depends on people high up on the religious ladder. People with wrong religious norms can spread unhappiness where ever they go. Also, a time may come in their own lives when they realize that they were dragged on a wrong path by the selfish religious zealots.

Religion is a two way sword. It can make you happy or it can make you a devil, a harbinger of death and destruction in some cases. As far as any individual is concerned, one should be able to choose one's own path towards good or bad norms. Unfortunately, this can be a hypothetical situation. One is sucked into the euphoria of religious extremists. Society will not allow you to select your path but will drag you toward the path of unhappiness and in some cases death and destruction.

The irony of the situation is, when one is dragged on a wrong path one may not even know it till it is too late. In short, religion by itself cannot make you happy, unless you have proper wisdom. Following the righteous path of religion along with your wisdom can lead you to eternal bliss. Many times, it is seen that the definition of eternal bliss changes from religion to religion. An obvious example is the mind-set of jihadists. Many of them think that the killing of those, who do not believe in their religion, can give one a permanent place in paradise or something like that. One may argue that such a jihadist when he dies during the process of killing others is completely at ease with oneself and sincerely thinks that he is going to the heaven. Such a crooked society, where norm for bliss is killing others, is not worth living in, unless you are a dumb person easy to be swayed on a wrong path by the religious extremists. If many of us choose to follow the path of a jihadist to acquire our eternal bliss, what type of the world will we be living in?— a world of dumb people massacring one another?

World Peace and Definitions of Morality, Virtues, and Vices

Religion is not the only venue that can lead the human race on an unhappy path, if not followed wisely and righteously. Think about politics. Extreme philosophies budding from the hidden selfish motives are equally dangerous. To start the war to line up the pockets of our friends and our vested companies is such an example. The unfortunate part is lax religious and political moral standards of the whole society as one unit dilutes the importance and influence of virtues. If everyone surrounding you is immoral then to be immoral becomes the norm of the society. Definitions of virtues and vices are reversed. The connection between success and happiness carried by virtuous particles only collapses. When such a situation occurs, the vices doing injustice to others will not create any unhappiness in such a society. As a result, people being oppressed by the injustice will become rebellious and violent, unless they have wise leaders to guide them effectively on a peaceful path. Efficacy of any philosophy employed by such leaders will be judged by the positive changes created in the lives of the oppressed people. Jingoism on the part of both, the oppressed and the oppressor, should be avoided in any case. This is not as difficult as it looks because all of them are the part of the same society. They may not have the same shared values initially, but slowly the situation can be rectified.

In this context, the thing to remember is the Happiness Index of the society, or the nation in general. People who came up with this index idea are wise, and so to say, practical philosophers. For some this term "practical philosophers" may be an oxymoron. For me, it is not, at least in the current context. What does this Happiness Index of the society tell us about this society where definitions of a virtue and a vice are interchanged? During the search of the answer, some obvious drawbacks are observed in the computation of this index. My opinion is: this Happiness Index has justified the situation previously described, "If everyone surrounding you is immoral then to be immoral becomes the norm of the society. Definitions of virtues and vices are reversed. The connection between success and happiness carried by virtuous particles only collapses."

In other words, the Happiness Index of the society is high even though the society has many vices. I do not mean that every society or nation that has a high Happiness Index is immoral. What I suggest here is there should be a universal definition of every critical virtue, the definition accepted by all human beings. Here, by definition, critical virtues are those when violated by one will adversely affect the happiness of others. The society has no right to be happy, if it is violating the accepted definitions of the critical virtues. Yet, when the whole society, as such, ignores this definition and receives a high Happiness Index—the situation somewhat troubles my consciousness. Here, I want to make myself clear that the original calculations of the index had nothing to do with virtues or vices in the society or the nation. That is all right—making the index true to what it measures. But what bothers me is it clearly shows, on a large scale such as the nation or whole society, that virtues have nothing to do with happiness, even when some vices are defined as virtues. This situation is detrimental to world peace. Talking in terms of the practical aspect of the above situation, it is very hard or sometimes impossible to reach a universal standard of morals and worldly accepted definitions of vices and virtues. Every nation or society exerts its self-bestowed right to adopt its moral standards and definitions whether we like it or not. This is acceptable, so long as it does not create any injustice to another society or country. As we always see, many conflicts and wars are caused by one party considering one's views morally superior to others. This is very apparent in terms of religious and political conflicts. It is, needless to say, all the religions try to teach to be virtuous. The problem, as we have noted earlier, is an interpretation of the religious scripts. Gone are the days when one could convert a person by the might of a sword—sword in one hand and the religious script in the other.

An attempt to convert another nation to one's political system using forceful means is equally naive. Such an attempt in this day and age will eventually fail. Every country has its own unique socio-economic problems or situations. Education level of the population, geography and history, to name a few, are the influential parameters in a study to decide religious and political systems of that country. By the strength of your military you may conquer the country, but you cannot convert its people to your political or religious system. You can take the horse to the water forcefully. That is all you can do. Permanent conversion is all together a new ball game. Therefore, a peaceful and patient infusion of your doctrines, your education standards, etc., is of prime importance. Otherwise, a forceful conversion is just a passing phase for that country and will be reversed as soon as the converting force is lifted. Also, it is a waste of time, money, and manpower of the converting nation.

Unfortunately, the human race is generally engaged in promoting one's own moral standards, religion, and definitions of virtues and vices. If we see around us, very few religious leaders are in a position to avoid global conflicts. That is, those who are religious are not powerful and those who are powerful may not be religious. Here, let me make it clear that religious leaders are those who teach their followers how to be successful and happy through virtues. This is the God's Philosophy they believe and practice. The religious leaders, who try to avoid global conflict, are not powerful leaders or cannot be powerful leaders. This is because the population at large bestows the power in political leaders who may have lax or selfish moral standards. This is a catch-22 situation: those, who are religious, are not powerful, and those, who are powerful, are not religious. Global conflict in this case can result in unhappiness stemming from death, destruction, economic suffering, etc. The political conflict is generally more devastating since the political leaders yield more power compared to the religious ones. The religious leaders are supposed to enhance the moral standard of the nation, but they are not powerful, so the situation can be resolved only by wise and virtuous political leaders who have already acquired the high moral standards under the coaching of the religious leaders. Such political leaders can very well increase the Happiness Index of the nation.

So far, we have seen that to result into happiness, success should be acquired through virtues. Also, the corollary is, happiness cannot be acquired without virtues. In what way is the latter statement tied to the Happiness Index of a society or a country? or is an individual happiness nothing to do with the happiness of the society? Obviously, the individual happiness must be included into the happiness of the society. The problem here is the difference between mass mentality and the mentality of an individual. A person of religion, other than yours, may be your good friend, but the same person in the company of his own religious extremists can be all together a different personality. One may often observe this situation in a daily life. Knowingly or unknowingly, the person adopts the moral and ethical standards of the mob. This totally changes his definitions of virtues and vices. This is the irony of the human race. Every society or nation may have its own norms which can create conflict with others.

When the conflict with another country or society arises, the Happiness Index will go down since it will affect the economic, mental, and physical wellness factors. Since the conflict is the result of no uniform definitions of virtues and vices, and since the Happiness Index is tied to the conflict, one may say that virtues and vices are automatically tied to the Happiness Index. For me, this is a very indirect way of connecting them. It does not take into account the agony of an individual caused by the sufferings of people from another country or society. As we have seen earlier, this is because of the difference between the mass mentality and that of an individual.

Thus, no matter how you look at the situation, it is imperative that all societies or countries should adopt uniform moral standards and definitions of those critical virtues and critical vices which have a potential to affect the happiness of other nations. This will eliminate the gap between mass mentality and individual thinking. Only then, will lasting peace and happiness prevail. It is a falsehood to think that since all the countries are happy, peace will prevail in the world. The world may be sitting on the time bomb of conflict between moral standards and nonuniform definitions of critical virtues and vices.

Revised Definition of GNH Number

(http://en.wikipedia.org/wiki/Gross_national_happiness also Executive White Paper by Med Jones of International Institute of Management http://www.iimedu.org/grossnationalhappiness/)

As the first global GNH (Gross National Happiness) survey has indicated, the GNH value is an index function of a total average per capita of the measures, given in the GNH Wikipedia These measures are very aptly selected by the wise and intelligent professors and philosophers. I am writing these measures here as given in Wikipedia. But their interpretation of influence on the true happiness of an individual is my own. In this context, I have divided the Wikipedia-listed measures into two groups. Group "A" is a primary one having a lot more impact or weightage on individual happiness compared to that of Group "B". These weightages will change based on the type of community or nation under study. Each measure has the parameters affecting its efficacy. These parameters are also very rational and cannot and should not be ignored. Here I give the list of Wikipedia measures and my classification either in Group A or Group B. Various parameters influencing these measures are also given here as listed in Wikipedia.

1. Economic Wellness Factor: This includes personal information of consumer debt, average income to consumer price index ratio and income distribution. This factor is in Group B.

2. Environmental Wellness Factor: Indicated via direct survey and statistical measurement of environmental metrics such as pollution, noise and traffic. This factor is in Group A.

3. Physical Wellness Factor: Indicated via statistical measurement of physical health metrics such as severe illness. This is in Group A.

4. Mental Wellness Factor: Indicated via direct survey and statistical measurement of mental health metrics such as usage of antidepressants and rise or decline of psychotherapy patients. This is in Group B.

5. Workplace Wellness Factor: Indicated via direct survey and statistical measurement of labor metrics such as jobless claims, job change, workplace complaints and lawsuits. This factor is in Group A.

6. Social Wellness Factor: Indicated via direct survey and statistical measurement of social metrics such as discrimination, safety, divorce rate, complaints of domestic conflicts and family

lawsuits, public lawsuits, crime rates. This is in Group B.

7. Political Wellness Factor: Indicated via direct survey and statistical measurement of political metrics such as quality of local democracy, individual freedom and foreign conflicts. This factor is in Group B.

8. As a thumb rule if we consider Group A to be twice influential to affect individual happiness compared to Group B, then their weightages can be calculated in terms of percentages as follows, "a" being percentile weightage factor of Group A and "b" being of Group B.

CHART 1

$$3a+4b=100$$
$$a=2b$$
$$6b+4b=100$$
$$b=10\%$$
$$a=20\%$$

Why I have selected this Group A or Group B for any individual Wellness Factor, needs my own clarification. A person who along with his family does not go hungry can be equally happy as some rich men. Up to certain limit of poverty, wealth has a little influence on individual happiness. The Environmental Wellness Factor has such parameters which may be considered as forces from the fifth dimension which are totally beyond the control of any individual and yet influencing his or her well-being.

Physical wellness is of prime importance and needs no further explanation.

Mental wellness is a subjective term. A state of mind for one person maybe his or her definition of happiness. This factor cannot be quantitatively defined. Many countries or societies have little or no psychologists or psychotherapist. As such, the influence of this factor on personal happiness should be considered as secondary.

Workplace wellness can amply influence a person's happiness. For example, an unemployed person can be seen happy in a very rare incidence, such as when the government takes care of the daily needs of the unemployed person and his family for an unlimited duration. If this situation prevails in the society then I will tend to consider Workplace Wellness Factor as Group B not Group A. Now recalculating the percentile weightage factors as follows:

CHART 2

$$2a+5b=100$$
$$a=2b$$
$$4b+5b=100$$
$$b=11.11\%$$
$$a=22.22\%$$

Social Wellness Factor influence is again very subjective. Out of the listed parameters, crime rate and safety can be considered as forces from the fifth dimension. The country or society where the crime rate is very high (that is to say, personal safety is greatly affected), this factor should be considered in Group A and not in Group B. This will recalculate percentile factors as follows:

CHART 3

$$4a+3b=100$$
$$a=2b$$
$$8b+3b=100$$
$$b=9.09\%$$
$$a=18.18\%$$

All the listed parameters in Political Wellness Factor have a secondary effect on the individual happiness. It is again noted here that the percentile weightages can vary from society to society or nation to nation. The above are just typical sample calculations.

"Time" and Historically Successful Personalities

If we take a pause and look at all the above factors and their parameters, it is easy to conclude that they can greatly influence all of us. It is very hard to find an individual who has totally escaped their influence. The only exception may be the personality of Fish Type 1, which has left the society in pursuit of pure wisdom. Such personalities are very rare and many times hidden from the society. The closest one I can come up with is The Buddha. But he was not of Fish Type 1 person. He was of Type 2 influenced by Environmental Wellness Factor. In the olden days, the king used to mold his citizenry. Nowadays, "Time" evolves the society and the society selects its leader. This line of thinking very easily helps me to conclude that "Time" creates exceptional personalities and not the other way round. "Time" is supreme and not the human being.

Time and again we see that when a country or a society is in a grave trouble, there may rise a personality to rectify the situation for all. We have seen such persons in US President Abraham Lincoln, Indian leader Mahatma Gandhi, United Kingdom Prime Minister Winston Churchill, US President Franklin Roosevelt, etc. If the country is not in trouble the traits of an exceptional person would remain dormant and people would not know much about his hidden qualities which made him a giant in history.

In fact, there could be many more such personalities who would have ably solved the then grave trouble the country was experiencing. It was a matter of luck that these great people were at right place and at right time. It was their destiny as depicted by the planetary positions in their horoscopes. Yet, we cannot take away their credit of tenaciously solving the critical problem of the country. The point here is that situation and circumstance at the time of trouble create the giant personality that solves the problem. In other words a personality does not create "Time"; "Time" creates the personality.

Examples of Lincoln, Gandhi, etc., are to the positive aspect of timely effect. The following story from the Hindu mythology covers the whole spectrum of the positive and the negative effects of "Time" factor on the entire life span. In the epic of "Mahabharata," Arjun was an exceptionally skillful warrior. Mostly because of his skills, the good guys Pandavas prevailed over the bad guys Kauravas in the Mahabharata war. When the war was over, the five Pandavas including Arjun left behind all their weapons and most of the worldly possessions and started the pilgrimage in the Himalayas. At one night, when they were sleeping under a tree, a few petty thieves stole their small remaining daily necessity—clothes, pots, and pans, etc. In the morning when the Pandavas got up, they knew they had nothing left. The author of the epic Mahabharata, sage Vyas, makes a point here: Think about the case of the great warrior Arjun. A time came in his life when the petty thieves were not afraid of him and successfully stole his remaining possessions. "Time" creates personalities and not the other way round. "Time" rules supreme.

Timing Versus the Nature of Success

Now coming to an individual success, does it mean that one should wait for the proper time to start the work towards one's success in life? Starting time for every project depends on the nature of the project. Scientists like Einstein started acquiring the knowledge of

Mathematics and Physics at a very early age. Then only he could discover the General Theory of Relativity. For a common man, who cannot achieve a spectacular success like *Einstein*, comes the theory of climbing multiple peaks as mentioned earlier. For him every time is a good time to climb successive peaks. This helps him to fully utilize his time and optimize the efficacy of his efforts to reach the properly selected peak. If these successive successes can be grouped together then eventually, may be in old age, the whole endeavor will result into one giant successful life.

Success in Adversities

When we are talking about the endeavor to achieve success, we have to remember that the human being is fallible. Also, adverse forces from the fifth dimension can set back one's plan to achieve success. Sometimes, the effect of such forces is devastating. One may feel very dejected. The sorrow of being treated so cruelly by luck, may break down one's morale completely. In this situation the best way to be successful is to work hard with deep concentration, so much so that one forgets one's miserable situation caused by the bad luck or by one's own follies.

I know the case of a student, who lost his one year of university education because of typhoid fever. All his friends and classmates were promoted to the next grade; whereas, he had to repeat his year. Instead of self-pity, this student studied so hard with great concentration that he had no time to think about his pitiable circumstances. The result was spectacular. It built his self-esteem which lasted throughout his life. He outshined his old classmates and friends all the time thereafter. It is up to every individual how to use one's adversities. The latter can show yourself a new you, a brilliant, tough side of you. When the going gets tough only the tough gets going. That can bring the best of any individual. Of course, different people react differently under a given situation. The hard work and concentration needed to be successful may vary from person to person. All are not born equal.

Not Born Equal, Yet Equal

Consider purely through the point of view of the situation at birth, say place (latitude and longitude) and time of birth, even though you may or may not believe in Astrology. The question is: Are all born equal that is with equal intelligence and equal brain power? The answer to me is "No". My consideration, apart from Astrology, is a practical one. I have seen some persons who can remember the text after reading it one time or twice while others have to read it many more times. At the same time, the first type of people may be such that they cannot understand mathematical subjects and tend to memorize the steps leading to the final mathematical answers. This is not a good situation to be for a good mathematician, which demands original thinking and not cramming the steps to solve the mathematical problem. The point is: some may be born with a good memory but with poor analytical skills. Others may have good mathematical skills but have poor memory.

I have read somewhere that a common man uses only ten percent of his brainpower. The difference of unequal brainpower at the time of birth can be easily overcome by hard work and concentration, that too at the early age of studentship. As Thomas Edison has said, "Genius is ninety percent diligence and ten percent intelligence". Though it may be a little exaggeration in some cases, the bottom line is there is a good scope of being successful in life, no matter with what intelligence or brainpower you are born with. In a given academic year, two students studying with the same number of hours and the same concentration power yet may score different grades. This is because one of them may have much better grasping power due to his hard work in his previous academic years. Intelligence and hard work accumulate during the course of time. The success in an undertaken endeavor depends on this cumulative intelligence and hard work. But as mentioned earlier, successive hard work with deep concentration can easily overcome the difference in intelligence or brainpower one is bestowed upon at the time of birth. Thus, one can achieve a spectacular success in life no matter what one is born with, (of course, with the exception of those who are badly maligned by the forces of the fifth dimension).

Happiness and "Line of Sight"

Success can result into happiness if the former is based on virtues, as we have seen earlier. This happiness can be long lasting depending on the orientation of your "line of sight". Using the theory of "Know Thyself", one may stop climbing various peaks of successful events. Then, if such a person has a downward angle for the line of sight, he will be happy. An upward angle will make him sad and/or jealous. A horizontal or level line of sight will make him "Sthitapradnya", a term used in the *Geeta* of Hindu script. The latter person is like a big commercial jetliner, no matter how the wind blows, it remains perfectly balanced. The phrase "line of sight" is borrowed from the story of three men—one, a teacher of prisoners in a penitentiary; the second one is a surveyor of property using Theodolite; and the third one is a shopkeeper.

The penitentiary teacher compares his own life with those of the prisoners who have miserable lives compared to his own. He is thankful to the Lord and feels happy for his own situation. The surveyor is accustomed to balance "line of sight" while taking the Theodolite readings. He is a wise man. He extrapolates his surveying procedure to his own daily life, does everything rationally, and thinks with controlled emotions. He is not perturbed by the adverse situation, nor gets carried away with joyous moments. He has perfectly balanced his "line of sight" while surveying a land or evaluating surrounding conditions in his daily routine. The shopkeeper, on the other hand, is always unhappy. He thinks that he is so poor compared to the other shopkeepers even though he works equally hard. He always compares himself to those who are better off than him. He looks at those who are higher up on the wealth ladder. His line of sight is always upward, resulting in self-pity and envy of others. So the central idea here is when one settles down in life one should look at those who are less fortunate and be happy, be thankful to the Almighty for making oneself more fortunate.

There is another anecdote about "line of sight". A person cannot afford a pair of shoes for his two feet. If he looks at people with shining shoes in their feet, he is unhappy. When he observes amputees with no legs he thanks god for giving him two legs. This makes him happy. A stage comes in everyone's life that he/she will not be happy unless he understands the theory of "Line of Sight".

God's Philosophy Based on Righteous Literature and Religious Mythology

In the above paragraph, I have invoked god. Many people do not believe in god. To me, the question, "if god exists or not" is redundant. Philosophy based on god is important. The philosophy does exist, whether it is based on a fictitious god or a real god does not matter to me. Many people consider, god as that person or authority who has created this universe. But for many, no one has created the universe. Universe is born or formed automatic by itself. In a religion, e.g. Hinduism, god is "Swayambhu" born from oneself. God is universe and universe is god. I consider myself to be a perfectly rational person, an outcome of science, engineering and technology. For me, god is not a myth but a hypothesis. A myth is something you believe in but cannot prove. Hypothesis can be proved indirectly but not by direct observations. We are discussing this "God's" business to answer the question: Does one's belief of god and/or his philosophy help to achieve success and happiness in life? My answer is: belief in god may or may not help but the philosophy based on god does help to reach one's goal successfully and be happy. In fact, the belief in the philosophy of god or god's philosophy can make one happy even though he or she may not be successful in life.

Once again, whether god exists or not is immaterial. God's philosophy gives us the answer to many riddles of life. Many times this philosophy is based on righteous literature and religious mythology. The latter tells us that there may be only one god or multiple gods. It does not matter how many. What matters is that god is an embodiment of virtues. If there are multiple gods in mythology, each god is an embodiment of certain virtue or virtues. When we worship god, indirectly we are worshiping those virtues. We ask the god to help us to inculcate those virtues in us. This is a good reminder to us that we have to learn these new virtues and practice them in our daily lives. If god exists or not and gives these virtues to us or not, does not matter. What matters is the creation of the inner urge to be virtuous by worshiping a believed or unbelieved god. Virtues can breed success in life, and success in life obtain through virtues can make one happy. God's philosophy gives us success and happiness through virtues. Worshiping god constantly or even intermittently reminds us to be virtuous and stay virtuous.

I have seen many examples in daily routine, how a sincere use of god's philosophy has a positive impact on a person's life. There was one student. He was very brilliant, and always topped every examination. One day, I happened to meet him. I asked him, how he could manage to maintain his topmost position. He took out from his wallet a piece of paper. That paper had ten stanzas from the religious scripts he specifically selected, appealing to him the most. He said that he had been reading these ten stanzas every day first thing in the morning. That guided him to the proper path of success throughout his day.

It is also not a surprise to see that percentage of successful people is more from the families where appropriate religious philosophies are nurtured using righteous literature and/or religious mythology. The aim of any religion should be to achieve success and happiness through virtues. Cultivate virtuous people, and success and happiness automatically follow. Of course, religion is not the only means to create a virtuous population. Law and order can force people to follow a virtuous or legal path. But virtues are something within, let's say intrinsic to a person. Law and order is something thrust on the society. Once the grip of law is released, the person or society in general may tend to practice illegal means full of vices. This does not happen with intrinsically virtuous people who acquired virtues through righteous literature or god's philosophy. No matter how you look at it, adherence to appropriate religious philosophy is the best means to achieve success and happiness for any individual or for a society/ country in general. Religious philosophy may not come from any one religion but may be adopted from many. Religion "A" may emphasize well the virtue "B", religion "C" may give better emphasis on virtue "D", etc. We should adopt the very best principles from any religion or literature to accelerate our progress towards success and happiness in life.

God and God's Philosophy for Lifelong Success and Happiness

I have heard a person saying, "I do not need god to remind me about virtues." Even a Nobel prize winning mathematician needs to be in touch with his subject. Otherwise, he may miss a few steps in solving some mathematical problems. It would be the same way, if a person does not constantly or at least intermittently remind oneself about virtues, he may adopt some sinful steps to be successful. Being in touch with god's philosophy or righteous literature can avoid these sinful steps. Also, I have heard a person saying, "In the past, I did not need to believe in god or in religious philosophy to achieve what I have today."

The flaw in this argument is that the person might have forgotten that someone else has inculcated in him the god's philosophy that helped him to be successful in life. This happening is based on the philosophical principle that children can enjoy the fruits of good-deed-trees planted by their parents. A person may not have any religious philosophical knowledge or nurtures but his parents have laid down the philosophical path he is walking on without him knowing that the path he is walking on is called the religious philosophical path.

It is a sheer ignorance on the part of such person to say that he did not need any religious philosophical help to achieve his success is life. He may augment his previous statement by saying, since he has achieved his goal; he has no need of god or god's philosophy in his current or future life. In this context one should remember what Edmond Hillary has said, "One cannot rely on laurels achieved a few years back." The fruit bearing tree by nature becomes barren in a due course of time. Above person may forget the virtues which helped him to be successful. Also, the path built by his parents for him may now be at its dead end. The net effect can lead to the diminishing returns of the success he has achieved in the past, or he may end-up like a person in the story of "The Nectar Pot".

So far, we have given the emphasis on the efficacy of god's philosophy affecting personal success and happiness, ignoring the belief in god himself. However, the latter has a special significance here. We know that the forces from the fifth dimension are beyond human control. Only god can exert any force in the fifth dimension. (Nuclear physicists and String theorists will excuse me for making this statement). As a result, the believers take refuge in the god to reduce or vile away the bad effect of the adverse fifth dimensional forces. The irony of this situation is, even the nonbelievers intend to invoke god, since they have no other defense against these adverse forces. It is of common observation that an atheist is praying for god to have mercy in a bad luck situation. Except in such a bad luck situation, the devotion towards god is cultivated step by step. It is not like a nuclear reactor where the controlled chain reaction is started just by inserting a Cadmium rod. Therefore, the belief in god and god's philosophy should be nurtured from an early age and thereafter continuously. Here we should remember that belief in god and/or knowledge of god's philosophy can be a major source of spiritual life which also includes your daily bound duties. In old age, when one loses partially or fully all the faculties of senses, such as hearing, eyesight, etc., then the devotion for god is of particular importance to develop inner peace and to prepare for the final journey from here to eternity. God and god's philosophy have a special role to play to bring happiness in that time span of human life. They bring inner peace and tranquility in a period when a human being is most vulnerable to the fear of old age ailments and death. Then, success or failure is history, happiness is the current entity. When a child is born, it cries while others are enjoying, laughing, and merrymaking. The same child as a grown up person when on the death bed, should have a smiling face, leaving the rest of the world crying over his demise. Belief in god and god's philosophy can help to achieve this.

"Just Do It"

Apart from the old age or severe handicap or illness situation, the greatest enemy working against success is working nothing towards success for the fear of failure. Here I will repeat that old statement, "We have nothing to fear but fear itself." We know Rome was not built in a day. The rate of success is always exponential. That is why we say, "Nothing succeeds like success." The only thing is, one has to follow the advice of the Nike Corp.—"Just do it." Select an aim appropriate to your situation and start working toward its success. Eventually, things will start falling in place. The initial path may be rough and full of hindrances. But be tough because as we have mentioned earlier, "When the going gets tough only the tough gets going." No one says that life is a bed of roses. But with smart efforts, one gets better and better in throwing away the thorns and leaving pure roses behind to enjoy. The theory of "Datum Level" is a special encouragement in this endeavor. The very thought of the players taking part in Special Olympics Games is the best encouragement to start working towards your lifelong goal.

Success and Smiling Heart

This is a good Earth. Success and happiness of an individual can make it better. Happiness spreads happiness. Unhappy people may spread gloom. How to be happy in life, how to keep the heart smiling even at adverse situations, is an art one should master. It is a sort of a psychological game played in solitude. One, who can master it, has a better chance of being successful, because, such a person can keep cool in an adverse situation. He is utilizing well his brainpower. People, who are dejected, feel gloomy in their hearts are unknowingly damaging their thinking faculties.

Gloom and sorrow eat up part of the brain. One loses concentration power. Energy is lost in self-pity. On the other hand, a person with smiling heart has automatically given smaller weightage to his miseries and the brain has a better capacity to concentrate and to think clearly.

Intensity and Duration of the Circle of Happiness

Success of an individual, apart from the personal Datum Level, can be measured by the length of radius of the Happiness Circle he has created around him. And the intensity of happiness can be measured by the field of success the person has adopted. Here is an illustration of the three successful personalities adopting three different fields of successful areas. The first person has built a successful drug pushing Mafia empire. He has made his drug pushers and drug addicts very happy by providing them narcotics in large quantities and on time. But this happiness is short-lived. They are all on the slippery slope of self-destruction. The second successful person has built his economic retail shop empire using all legal and virtuous means. This has made his shareholders rich and materially happy. But this may not ease their day-to-day problems, unless there is a cultivation of inner sense of satisfaction without a trace of greed. Of course, we do not blame the successful retail shop empire builder, if the rich shareholders are unhappy. Yet, we have to understand that there is less intensity of happiness in the shareholders' community compared to the one illustrated in the third example. The third successful person is a saint, who has shown by his own selfless work, how to be happy and self-contained in what you have, and at the same time work for a bigger and better achievement in life that too adopting all virtuous means. Here I want to make clear that a contented person may work for further success provided he is not perturbed by its failure. By these three examples, it is easy to see that the intensity and duration of happiness spread by these three successful people varies, and based on the field in which the success is achieved. Thus, in summary, the measure of success is the length of radius of the Happiness Circle. The intensity of happiness spread around depends on the field of success selected by the successful personality.

In light of the above discussion, it may be clear that one should try for an aim which will increase the radius of the Happiness Circle around oneself. A mayor of a big city has a better scope to spread happiness in a bigger area, compared to a school teacher in that city. This is not to show that a school teacher's job is no good. The example means to say that one should aim high to be in a position to spread happiness in a larger area. The field of success selected should create as large as possible the happiness intensity in the area defined by the radius of the Happiness Circle. Here I want to make it clear that the theory of "Line of Sight" is applicable when one settles in life and not when one is in a process of selecting one's aim of life.

The subjects selected to be successful in can be broadly classified as, spiritual, material, physical, and daily routine type. The example of the saint illustrates the spiritual subject. The material one is that which spreads the economic prosperity. The physical success, such as in sports, can have a large radius of happiness spread around, for example, an Olympian winning many gold medals, making the whole country happy. The daily routine areas are something like politics, science, technology, medicine, etc. The duration and intensity of happiness spread by these fields of success can vary considerably. The aim of life is to maximize the area of the Happiness Circle and also its intensity and duration.

Social Obligations toward "Forgotten" and "Downtrodden"

In a society or a country, there are pockets of the population, which are out of all the Happiness Circles. Here, you have a high probability of finding unhappy people. These people are divided into two categories: Those under the adverse influence of the forces from the fifth dimension termed as the "Downtrodden", and secondly, those who are miserable by their own deeds due to the lack of spiritual knowledge or understanding of god's philosophy. I will call this second group as the "Forgotten". Both these groups need external help but only the Downtrodden deserve it. The Forgotten should be helped by their own community leaders. The moral and ethical standards tell us that we should help everyone who is in misery. It is easier said than done. How far is it practical to implement this philosophy?

In practice, people in the Happiness Circle, by the nature of the human being, are reluctant to help others. Their stereotype thinking is: Who cares for the GNH number, so long as I am happy! A small fraction of the happy people willing to help may do so in terms of charity donations and government taxes imposed upon them. Almost no one is willing to donate man-hours for social work, maybe because they are overwhelmed by their own daily working hours.

Charity donations are uncertain and government taxation is a political football. All election philosophies are based on it. Therefore, the financial aid to improve the lot of the Downtrodden and the Forgotten is very uncertain. Many people aptly think: What percentage of this economic aid is used for the true upliftment of the people it is meant for? Their skepticism can be justified in many ways. However, it is their bounden duty to help the Downtrodden no matter what. It is morally, ethically, and spiritually demanded. A question comes about the Forgotten. These are the people who do not deserve any external help, but as a mercy should be helped economically. The only definite way for the Forgotten to improve their community GNH is by self-help. If they get external monetary help it will be a frosting on the cake. It is the duty of the community leaders of the Forgotten to guide them on god's philosophical path. If the leaders fail to do so, they do not deserve to be leaders. Also these leaders should help the Downtrodden of their community and see that the external monetary help through charities and taxation is properly utilized.

The root cause of suffering, miseries, and unhappiness in any community is lack of proper leadership. The conflict between the haves and the have-nots, the oppressor and the oppressed, the rulers and the ruled, etc, is a historical fact. Except the "Tasaday Tribe" all the human beings should have understood this long time back and found out the solution for this situation. The successful implementation of the solution may take a varied duration depending on the graveness of the conflict. The point here is: The leaders of the Downtrodden and the Forgotten should understand this age-old conflict and find the way to tackle it. It is too late to use this conflict as an excuse for the status quo or lack of progress in their communities. The happiness and success of any community can be greatly affected by the deeds of its leaders.

As we have mentioned earlier, unhappy are those who deserve to be unhappy, barring those who are very mercilessly treated by the forces of the fifth dimension. We are now talking about Forgotten who are miserable because of their own ineptness. The main reason for their misery is a lack of understanding of god's philosophy. They may believe in god, they may be very devotional, but they have no comprehension of god's philosophy. The most important principle is: One should be virtuous, void of all vices, and try one's at-most to uplift oneself. Many people try to improve their lots by adopting sinful methods full of vices. Such people are on the slippery slope of destruction and eventually fall into the abyss. Their self-destruction is quick and complete. The population in the Happiness

Circle watches this downfall. The onlookers in general may ignore this phenomenon, considering it to be none of their business. Can we justify this behavior? My answer is "Yes". Please remember here that we are talking about those who lack spiritual bases (main source of which is god's philosophy, as stated earlier), also, who are not subjected to the forces from the fifth dimension, and who select their own slippery slopes by adopting sinful and viceful methods. It is the bounden duty of their leaders to imbibe appropriate virtues in such people. Since these leaders may lack economic and other means to help their followers, initial progress can be slow. At this juncture it is beneficial for the people in the Happiness Circles to help these leaders in their efforts of spiritually as well as mentally uplifting the brothers on the slippery slopes.

Vices of any sector of a society are a nuisance for the whole society. It can result in building more prisons than the building of more education institutes. Prisons teach vices. Many times, the prisoners coming out of prison after completing their sentences are more sinful compared to when they entered the prison. This further increases their probability of entering the prison again. This is an endless chain reaction. In this context, it is easy to see that measure number six "Social Wellness Factor" of the first GNH (Gross National Happiness) will adversely affect the overall happiness of the society or nation.

It is needless to list here all the possible vices in the society. But the first vice that comes to my mind is "scant respect for virtues". It is obvious that if the people have no respect for virtues, why should they be virtuous? In such society, teen pregnancies, divorce rates, family lawsuits, school dropouts, crime rate, etc., are all progressively rising unless checked by the respective community leaders properly aided by the people in the Happiness Circles.

The Above discussion is for the Forgotten, the unhappy people who deserve to be unhappy since their unhappiness is due to their own follies and not by the influence of the forces from the fifth dimension. Now what about those who are truly the downtrodden through no fault of their own, but by the destiny or luck factor? Such persons, in general can be small kids, ladies oppressed in their families and/or society, invalids, old people, etc. Their horoscopes got them into this category. They cannot uplift themselves on their own. At this stage, some Women's Liberals will object for including Women in this category. But my observation is: Women in Downtrodden societies, some third world countries, in religious zealot societies/ countries, definitely fall in this vicious situation. Their surroundings are too adverse for them and badly need external help. The irony of the situation is: Their own community leaders and family members who are supposed to help them are the main oppressors. The fence of a farm that is supposed to guard the crop is itself destroying the crop.

Kids following wrong path are not to be blamed, but the blame goes to the sinful environment around them. They are just the puppets in the hands of destiny. Their planetary situations at the time of their births have destined them to be so. Who is going to help them?

Or will they walk on the slippery slope of vices and end up in the penitentiaries, reducing the Social Wellness Factor and in general, the overall GNH number of the society or nation? These kids need help from all those who are in a position to help in any form of actions and words. That will definitely enhance the GNH number of the society or nation. Leaving these kids to their fates or to the mercy of their family members is a grave folly. In fact, the family environment and upbringing are the reasons for the miseries of these kids. The path of correcting the family members first with the hope that they will help their kids is very roundabout way of helping the kids. Probability of its success is small. It is time consuming and meanwhile, the kids may be on the slippery slopes of vices. Direct help to the kids is of the essence here. The time factor demands it.

It is said that any society is judged by the way it treats its elders and invalids. These elders and invalids are in all strata of the society and should be aptly taken care of by the remaining populace. This greatly influences the Mental and Social Wellness Factors of GNH number for the society/nation. In short, it is the bounden duty of the whole society to uplift Downtrodden. The Forgotten should uplift themselves. Also a major role in doing so should be played by their community leaders.

Gross National Success (GNS)

So far we have discussed individual success and happiness, and also the happiness of the community or nation in general. In the same token, I have come up with the criteria of Gross National Success (GNS) which can be applied to the community or a whole nation. The success can be measured for a given duration, e.g. every year or for a given generation period (say thirty years), or for a duration of a given president's rule, etc. The GNS number constitutes many "Success Factors" (SF) and each factor has some variable parameters. The "Success Percentile" (SP) for each parameter is calculated as (Ne-Nb)x100/Nb. Nb is the parameter value at the beginning of the measurement period, Ne is at the end of it. Then the average (SPavg) of these SP values is calculated for every SF.

"Weightage Success Factor" (WSF) for every SF is decided based on the type of community or nation. The sum of maximum possible Weightage Success Factors (WSF) is 100. Detailed computations of WSF are given in the example below. The above calculated SPavg is a percentile number (i.e. out of 100). It is then converted to the value out of WSF for that SF item. This number is called "Final Success Factor" (FSF). Summation of all these FSF is the final Gross National Success (GNS) number of that community or nation for the particular measurement period. The larger the number, the more successful is the nation or the community in that selected time period.

The above calculations may look tedious. In fact, they are not, as illustrated in the following example. Please note that the various Success Factors and their parameters are selected as preliminary entities. Learned sociologists, philosopher, psychologists, and other wise persons should update these parameters and factors. They are better judges for these selections.

The sample calculations are given here. In this example w1, w2 and w3 are the three Weightage Success Factors (WSF) used. W1 WSF is the largest used for intercommunity or international SF. Science, Technology and Economic SF's have w2 WSF. The smallest w3 is given for Social, Environmental and Physical SF's. These Weightages are arbitrarily selected.

Computation of Gross National Success (GNS)

Science and Technology Success Factor:

Science and Technology parameters are

Number of papers published, Success Percentile, SP =A1%

(Note that A1= (Ae-Ab) x100/Ab, where Ab is beginning number of papers published and Ae its value at the end of the measurement period)

Number of research and educational institute, SP =A2%

|

Etc.

Science and Technology Success Factor, SF = Average of A1, A2, etc, Spavg=Aavg%

Selected Science and Technology Weightage Success Factor, WSF=w2

Science and Technology Final Success Factor, FSF= (Aavgxw2)/100

Economic Success Factor:

GNP Success Percentile SP =B1%

Balance of Trade SP=B2%

Personal Income SP =B3%

Unemployment Rate SP =B4%

|

Etc.

Economic Success Factor SF=Average of B1, B2, B3, B4—etc SPavg=Bavg%

Selected Economic Weightage Success Factor WSF = w2

Economic Final Success Factor FSF= (Bavgxw2)/100

Intercommunity or International Success Factor :

Number of Wars engaged SP=C1%

Number of Wars stopped between two countries SP=C2%

Number of Countries helped in their calamities SP=C3%

|

Etc.

War Success Factor SF =Average of C1, C2, C3, etc.=Cavg%

Selected War Weightage success Factor WSF=w1

War Final Success Factor FSF= (Cavgxw1)/100

Social Success Factor:

Crime Rate Success Percentile SP =D1%

High School Graduate SP =D2%

Divorce Rate SP=D3%

Teen Age Pregnancy SP=D4%

Domestic Conflict and Family Lawsuits SP=D5%

|

Etc.

Social Success Factor SF = Average of D1, D2, etc
SPavg =Davg%

Selected Social Success Weightage Factor WSF=w3

Social Success FSF= (Davgxw3)/100

Environmental Success Factor:

Pollution Success Percentile SP=E1%

Noise and Traffic SP=E2%

|

Etc.

Environmental Success Factor SF = Average of E1, E2, etc Spavg=Eavg%

Selected Environmental Success Weightage factor WSF=w3

Environmental Final Success Factor FSF= (Eavgxw3)/100

Physical and Mental Success Factor:

Severe illness SP=F1%

Usage of antidepressant SP=F2%

|

Etc.

Physical and Mental Success Factor SF = Average of F1, F2, etc Spavg=Favg%

Selected Physical and mental success weightage factor WSF =w3

Physical and Mental Final Success Factor FSF= (Favgxw3)/100

The major difference between GNH and GNS, apart from various "Factors," is the way weightage factors are calculated. While doing so emotions or personal feelings play a small role in GNS compared to the one in GNH. Also GNS is measured from the

"Datum Level" of the parameter value at the beginning of the measurement period. Consider the following sample calculations for Weightage Success Factors (WSF) of certain nation.

W1=3xw3
W2=2xw3
Since the summation of WSF is 100, we have
w2+w2+w1+w3+w3+w3 =100
2w2+w1+3w3=100
4w3+3w3+3w3=100
10w3=100
W3=10
W1=30
W2=20

Using these w1, w2 and w3 Weighted Success Factors WSF, the Final Success Factors are calculated for the six success factors from science and technology to physical and mental success factors. Then the required GNS number of that community or nation for the designated period (e.g. four years period of a given president), is computed as:

GNS=FSF1+FSF2+FSF3+FSF4+FSF5+FSF6

As a numerical example consider a nation whose 4 years measurement period has the following average Success Percentile SPavg for the respective success factors from Science and Technology to Physical and Mental Success Factors.

CHART 4

ITEM\SF #	1	2	3	4	5	6
SPavg	70	40	60	30	20	50
Calculated WSF	w2=20	w2=20	w1=30	w3=10	w3=10	w3=10
FSF=(SPavg X WSF)/100	14	8	18	3	2	5

$$GNS = SFSF = 14 + 8 + 18 + 3 + 2 + 5 = 50$$

The larger the GNS number, the more successful is the country or community in that period. It is noted here that the success percentile "SP" is negative for the terms like wars, crime rate, severe illness, etc., in case they show increase in a given measurement period. This should show reduction in the success of the community/nation. It is further noted that in a diverse country there may be many different communities. If needed, these diverse communities can be given their own "SP" values for the same item under consideration, while calculating the GNS number for that community.

Paradigm Shift in GNH Weightage Factors

This discussion leads us to the extreme paradigm shift situation, which is particularly seen in Gross National Happiness (GNH) number of a community or a nation. I have observed such communities, particularly in the underdeveloped countries. If we do not account for these paradigm shifts, GNH does not represent the true state of happiness of that developing community or country. When I was thinking about these communities, I observed extreme paradigm shift in the weightages of various GNH factors and their parameters. It is of a common observance that many rich people lack the comprehension of empathy which is an ability to understand fellow-feelings particularly of those at the lower strata of the society. Also, the ultra-rich people may have lost the faculty of savoring the daily simple pleasures of life. Excess of any good thing can reduce its importance and lessen the pleasure derived from it. I remember those days before TV era was born. We used to enjoy watching movies. It was a special treat. It is no more so now. A materially deprived community with mutual trust and cooperation is observed to exist happily. The community members share their joys and sorrows, so to say; they have a good judgment of empathy. For such community economic wellness factor should have zero weightage to describe its GNH accurately. The Social Wellness Factor has the major influence on its high GNH number. The rest of the weightages have very limited contribution (positive or negative) to the final GNH value.

To explain this drastic shift in the weightage factor, one should study the parameters constituting the Social Wellness Factor. These parameters such as discrimination, divorce rates, domestic conflicts, etc., are almost nonexistent in this virtuous society. If some individual ignores these virtues, he will be thrown out of the society. There is a self-cleansing mechanism in place. Many people may think that I am describing some Utopian society or community here. So, let me give some details of this society. These are the small farmers and farm-hands living in the villages. They get enough food to eat and in case of famine, the government helps them. They believe in god and also in god's philosophy very sincerely, and yet they are not fanatics. They are tolerant to other religions in the community. They are satisfied with what they possess. They get great pleasure to be one with the nature, e.g. chit-chatting under starry night, watching the monsoon rainfall, sitting around an open air campfire in the winter night, etc. Their addictions are somewhat harmless and not expensive, such as locally available in abundance the chewing or sniffing of tobacco. Very often occurring during religious festivals and fairs, these are sources of immense pleasure. Open fields and forests, and no concrete jungles add happiness to their daily life. No overdependence on machinery or electric/electronic gadgetry creates less complication in a simple and smooth joyous routine. Unpolluted air of open fields and forests results in healthy and long living generations. Such a community should show a high value of GNH. If any, the nation has pockets of such communities then their presence should be properly reflected in the overall GNH of the nation.

Part 2
The Theory of "Happism"

This study of success and happiness leads me to the following theory of *Happism* aimed at permanent and sustainable happiness on Planet Earth. If the powers and the superpowers in UNO try sincerely, then they can create permanent peace and heaven on earth by adopting this theory for the world nations. Apparently, some of the *Happism* considerations given here may seem drastic for the current world stage. But, a drastic situation needs a drastic solution, particularly when there are no other remedies. The French Emperor Napoleon Bonaparte has said, "There is no word like *impossible* in my dictionary." We can do it. Otherwise, I am sure the human race will be forced to adopt this theory in some form or the other, in a due course of time. That time rather be now than later. This is a critical juncture in the history of the human race. Any delays in adaptation will drift the situation from bad to worse to irreversible.

The following manifesto is dedicated to the eternal peace and happiness of all living beings on Planet Earth.

Manifesto of Happism

The People and the leaders of each and every nation must take an oath to uphold the following Considerations.

1. *Population Consideration*:

Every nation is allocated its Allowable Population Quota (APQ), which is the larger of the following (a) and (b) numbers.

Allowable Population Quota = Half of the current population of the nation, Allowable Population Quota = (Total square mile area of the nation) X 10, i.e. maximum allowable population density is 10 per square mile

Every country must enforce the rule of "One woman one child" till it trims down its population to its APQ level. Once the population reaches APQ the rate of child birth will be permanently locked at Zero Population Growth (ZPG) rate. Note that, if a nation chooses, its population can be below APQ, but never more. Also, if the nation chooses, immigration is allowed subjected to the condition that total population does not exceed APQ.

2. *Border Consideration*:

Borders of all the nations are frozen permanently to the current state.

3. *Weapon Consideration*:

The weapon arsenal of any nation is frozen to its current level. No nation is allowed to develop any new weapon system nor allowed to increase the quantity of weapons it possesses already. Weapon production is limited to the level required for internal law and order usage. Exporting of the weapons is allowed, subjected to the condition that weapon importing nation uses it strictly for establishing its internal law and order situation and not for any foreign aggression.

4. *Science and Technology Research Consideration:*

All the research work on science and technology will be permanently stopped except in the areas of Allowable Research Field (ARF), such as medicine, pharmacy, agriculture, horticulture, Global Warming and Green Earth. Current technical and scientific knowledge of the human race is enough to keep it happy, particularly when its population is only half. Extra knowledge is redundant and waste of money and manpower. Savings in these fields should be diverted to the areas of ARF. Thus, the scientific and technical knowledge is frozen to the respective current level of that nation. The nation may improve its theoretical knowledge to the maximum current level human race has attained. But the experimental and testing works are permanently banned except in ARF areas.

5. *Production Consideration:*

The manufacturing capacity, production level and acquisition of raw materials are frozen to the respective current states of a give nation. Based on demand and supply, the nation may reduce but never surpass these respective current states. Also, there will be unrestricted imports and exports of raw materials and manufactured goods between world nations. This implies that if some country wants advanced scientific gadgetry it can import it rather than trying to develop it on its own. By this arrangement the country will spare its population from learning any practical application of scientific and technical knowledge more than what it knows currently.

6. *Religious Consideration:*

All religions and their leaders must respect and be tolerant of other religions. There will be a complete freedom for an individual to follow any religion that greatly emphasizes virtues and nothing but virtues. No attempt of religious conversions is permitted. God's philosophy of success and happiness through virtues will be vigorously, judiciously, and constantly followed.

7. *Environmental Consideration:*

Every nation and its leaders must improve its environment such as quality of air and water, acreage of forest land, etc. It should not be a big task as the population is only half, production is reduced, and a large number of scientists and technocrats are working toward agriculture, horticulture and Green Earth research of ARF areas.

If a country refuses to follow these considerations then that country will cease to exist. It will be divided into surrounding countries based on the lengths of common borders. An island nation will be absorbed in its nearest country. This task will be carried out by the rest of the world nations working together.

Since this conflict will be one rogue nation against rest of the world, it will be an easy and a short-lived task. It is further noted here that to be permanently and sustainably happy, the steps to be followed by all the nations, rich or poor, are the same. I am very optimistic. There is nothing impossible for the human race. It can easily adopt these considerations and bring permanent and sustainable happiness on Earth. However, some initial obstructions are expected during the execution of this theory of *Happism*. A summary of these obstructions is given in the following section.

Obstructions in Happism Theory Implementation

1. *Delay in Population Control*

   This delay is very detrimental for the success of the theory since the whole mathematical consideration of the theory is based on the population quota of any nation. All the nations must immediately and simultaneously work on reaching their respective Allowable Population Quota (APQ) number. Mother Earth is already overburdened by the human race.

2. *Fanatic and/or Selfish Religious Leaders*

   To increase the number of their followers such leaders tend to convert others. Economic enticement or brute force may be used during the conversion. In that case the Social Wellness Factor; and therefore, the GNH number of the nation is bound to go down. As we have stated earlier, the main function of any religion is to teach how to achieve success and happiness through virtues. This is a fundamental principle of god's philosophy. The fanatic and/or selfish religious leaders defy this teaching. Such religious leaders should be identified by the public and immediately defrocked.

3. *Selfish Political Leaders*

To divert the attention of the population from the internal political turmoil, some of the leaders pick up fights with adjacent nations. Some political leaders simply do not comprehend the importance of various considerations of *Happism*. People of the nation should remove such leaders from power. Otherwise these leaders will lead the nation astray. Eventually, such nation will not obey the *Happism* consideration and will be attacked by the rest of the world. This setback to *Happism* will be short-lived since rest of the world with joint efforts will tackle the rogue nation very easily and quickly.

4. *Astray Scientists and Technocrats*

Since by the principle, *Happism* theory diverts all the scientific and technical research towards ARF areas, the scientist and technocrats working in the areas other than ARF may resent this. Such scientists and technocrats should be treated sympathetically and their talents be utilized in ARF works as much as possible.

5. *Arrogant and/or Expansionist nation*

A nation trying to dominate the world or surrounding nations by its military might will have scant respect for world peace. A land grabbing nation will not like the borders frozen permanently at the current level. Sometimes, these border claims maybe legitimate but the legitimacy is very subjective. Also, there is no limit to such claims. A better way is to freeze the borders for good.

6. *Jealous Nation*

A certain nation can be behind others in some considerations e.g. weaponry. Such nation may not like the clause of Weapon Consideration, as a result, will oppose *Happism*. But this nation should remember that any effort to catch up with other nations is an open-ended, never ending competition, and it's better to be stopped at the current level.

7. *Distrust among Different Factions*

This is the most damaging cause acting against the success of *Happism*. The differences among religions, political systems, races, skin colors, etc., can be the main culprits. Religious and political leaders are to play active roles to correct this situation. For this reason check and counter-check committees should be in place. A check committee is for a given nation made up of its own citizens to check that the above *Happism* considerations are properly upheld. There should be a separate check committee for each consideration, made up of experts in that consideration field. Then there should be a counter-check committee for each consideration, made up of foreign citizens. For example, Consideration 1, Population Consideration, Counter-Check Committee of nation "A" will consist of citizens from nations B, C, D, E, etc., who have no vested interests in the nation "A". Then any Counter-Check Committee of say nation "B" should not include any citizen from the nation "A". This is to avoid any unholy alliance between nations "A" and "B".

Critical Time to Implement Happism

This is a critical time period in the history of human race to start implementing this theory of *Happism*. We have already reached the scientific and technical level to make us happy, particularly, when our population will be only half of the current one. The same is true for our production capacity and know-how. Any more effort in these areas is simply a waste of time and energy, a waste of brainpower. It will not add anything extra to the happiness of the human race. On the other hand, acquiring advanced scientific and technical knowledge needs sacrifice of youthful years. Enjoy the Green Earth in that period, instead of sitting in a classroom or on a study table. It makes a big difference in happiness also in savoring the every day pleasures of life.

Emphasis on Allowable Research Fields (ARF) will accelerate the beauty of the environment. A controlled manufacturing to the minimum level will be needed, since the population is only half, and will reduce the emission of detrimental gases. Global warming will be nonexistent. Skies will be blue, nights will be starry, stream waters will be transparent clean, mountains and hills will be green with lush forests, abundant animals and birds will live in harmony with the human race. That is the happiness in life, as against the pseudo-pride in one's religion or military might of one's nation.

After all, we should always remember, "How much land does a man need?" as Count Leo Tolstoy has asked. A young man busy in amassing wealth, getting wealthier and wealthier, and then realizing after a certain time that he is now an old man and has no time to enjoy his own hard-earned wealth. This thing should not happen with the human race. This is the optimum time in human history that we should enjoy the fruits of our hard-earned scientific and technical knowledge, instead of toiling for more, as the man did in the Tolstoy story. This is the prune time to apply midcourse correction in our efforts toward acquiring wealth and non-ARF knowledge. Success will be measured in terms of happiness and nothing but happiness.

I feel our scientists and technocrats have brought the human race at the correct juncture though I would have preferred: this scientific and technical progress was to occur when human population was half of the current one. Still it is not too late and we should be thankful to these scientist and technocrats for what they have achieved for us all.

Failures of Religious and Political Leaders

Unfortunately, we cannot say the same thing about our religious and political leaders. Many religious leaders are not successful in controlling the fanatics, or better to say, in some cases they have created the fanatics. They have not understood the importance of population control. They have fomented all the religious wars, fights among neighbors, oppression of women, created terrorists, etc. Very few religions and religious leaders are successful in avoiding these pitfalls. It is the duty of any religious leader to be tolerant to other religions, create virtuous disciples and bring peace and tranquility to the community and nation in general.

Political leaders should remember that every nation has its peculiar history, geography, culture, religion, etc. A virtue in one system can be a vice in another. Though this situation is not desired, *Happism* allows it to some extent for non-critical virtues; so long as it does not trouble other nations. It is no good to impose one's own political system on another nation. A nation may or may not know its limitations, but it may try to learn about them. Eventually, such a nation adopts itself to be happy in a political system forced by its own leaders. Leave such a nation to its own trial and error process; as long as it does not create any problem for others. This will be its test to show if it is a nation of Type 3 or Type 4 fish personalities. The failure of religious and to some extent political leaders has made difficult the task of implementing *Happism* successfully. However, I am optimistic that the rest of the world will come together and help to create permanent and sustainable happiness on Earth.

Time and again we have seen the connection between individual success and the success of the whole community or nation. Recent examples are of US President Abraham Lincoln, Indian leader Mahatma Gandhi and United Kingdom Prime Minister Winston Churchill to name a few. Time uplifted their dormant personalities. To implement *Happism*, we should adopt Nike's principle "Just do it." We have mentioned in previous pages how opportune "Time" can create such historic personalities. We should just try sincerely to execute *Happism* and "Time" will create such Lincolns, Gandhis and Churchills. We have to create a new world order. Originally a few, then more, then still more people will join this endeavor. We should not feel dejected for the current political and religious conditions of the world. The required personalities and leaders will be created by "Time" if we give "Time" a chance by our own efforts.

Happism and Specific Case Studies

In this section we will study a few ancient and modern communities to guide us during an implementation of *Happism*. These examples emphasize the importance of god's philosophy, environment, "Inclusive and Exclusive" nature of happiness, etc. They also show that further advancements in science and technology will not enhance human happiness once the other onsiderations of *Happism* are in place.

If we look at the human history, we see people enjoying real happiness at the juncture where population number, god's philosophy, environment, and scientific progress were in perfect balance and harmony. It was immaterial that people were scientifically primitive compared to today's standard. Such examples are abundant in the countries with ancient civilizations. These civilizations were based on god's philosophy which made them happy in spite of their primitive living.

What about those historical examples where there were more urban developments through science and technology, e.g., some cities in Roman Empire? Probably, the people were happy too. We may further argue that the abovementioned old civilizations including the Roman Empire eventually vanished. What is the difference between the two? The Roman Empire ceased to exist because of its own decadence, void of god's philosophy, and maybe by the enemies it created by its own expansionist's tendency. Old civilizations vanished because of the forces from the fifth dimension, e.g., the outside barbarian attacks. If the outside people were civilized (which implies obeying god's philosophy), there would have been internal peace and happiness which we are striving for through *Happism*.

There is no doubt that the human race and its uncontrolled population growth, along with the rampant manufacturing plants to satisfy the insatiable thirst of material goods, has ruined our environment. Remember those days in the recent past where beautiful rivers were flowing all the twelve months of the year. Now riverbeds downstream of the dams are all dry. We need dams to irrigate our crops. We need bumper crops to feed our uncontrolled population. So, we have ruined the nature by drying the riverbeds. Talk to those people who are so unhappy to see their beautiful rivers being converted to open drainages. Population explosion is the main culprit and the necessary technical means to sustain it is the secondary one, in ruining the happiness derived from the beautifully flowing rivers.

Now, think of the stockbrokers in Wall Street area. They may be materially happy. For them, living in concrete jungles is real happiness. If you have not seen something, you don't miss it. For example, people in remote villages, who have never seen a TV, will never miss it. In this context, we have to remember that we are talking about the happiness of the whole nation and about the execution of *Happism*. Therefore, it is essential to use different Weightages of a given factor for different communities (e.g., brokers, farmers, etc.), in a nation while deriving its GNH number. The *Happism* Theory accounts for these variations in the source of happiness.

When we read above two paragraphs what we see that the happiness of the stockbroker and of the villager who has not seen the TV, are mutually exclusive, that is one does not derive the happiness at the cost of the other. Therefore, we should leave alone the stockbroker and the villager to enjoy their respective environments. However, we should understand that only a limited number of people can enjoy stock exchange wealth but the wealth of nature is unlimited. Yet, both these situations are perfectly acceptable to *Happism*, since they are mutually exclusive. Now consider the happiness of the people getting bumper crop and unhappiness of people living downstream of the dam where the river is turned into an open drainage. Happiness of one and unhappiness of other are mutually inclusive, that is they cannot be separated. One is the cause of the other. As Abraham Lincoln has said, "You cannot enrich the poor by pooring the rich." Here we have ruined the happiness of downstream people to enrich the happiness of the upstream ones. That is against what Lincoln has stated and what *Happism* expects. The measure should uplift the happiness of all and not of one at the cost of the other.

Nobel Prize Recommendations

It is abundantly clear that once our population is held steady at APQ level, we do not need any more advances in science and technology except in ARF area. Also, to accelerate ARF progress, we need to channel human brilliance, which is saved from further research in science and technology. We should eventually eliminate giving Nobel Prizes in Physics, Chemistry, and Mathematics. While doing so, we should properly reward the past and the current hard work done by these scientists. We should show our utmost respect for their work. It may take a little more than one generation for this elimination. But the corresponding date should be announced well in advance. At the same time we should announce new areas of awarding Nobel Prizes. These areas will obviously be related to ARF, population control, spreading god's philosophy, etc.

Justification of Brute Force

It is further noted here that we have recommended a brute force as a final resort against the nation which refuses to join the successful execution of *Happism*. Is this brute force justified? Yes, it is because any violation of the *Happism* consideration is against the rest of humanity. Consider the following examples: increase in population over Allowable Population Quota (APQ) recommended by number 1 Population Consideration, causes extra burden on Mother Earth. Also, it may have a hidden agenda of creating religious and political hegemony concealed under the garb of extra population. Violating number 3, Weapon Consideration results in creating an endless chain reaction of weapon competition. Thus, the case can be made against the violation of every consideration, giving the rest of the world a moral right to use might against such a vagabond nation. If the rest of the world is perfectly united against that one nation, the conflict will be short-lived and peace and happiness will prevail soon.

Environmentalists as Friends of Happism

Work of environmentalists and *Happism* execution go hand in hand. Environmentalists alone may try hard to stop further destruction of nature. But their efforts will be too short and too late in the absence of *Happism*. Glaciers will melt, rain forests will be cut, concrete jungles will expand, and acid rains will fall unless the *Happism* Theory is implemented. Human race is smart but selfish. It knows all these consequences. But because of its selfish efforts in wrong directions, it creates the illusion that these are unavoidable natural disasters. Or better to say, human race skillfully augments these disasters to fulfill its selfish motives by deliberately avoiding *Happism* Considerations. But enough is enough; this is a perfect time to adopt the *Happism* Theory for permanent and sustainable happiness on Earth. Let us recruit environmentalists to help us in this regard.

Pockets of Happiness in Chaotic Surroundings

We have seen earlier, that there are some communities which have been enjoying happiness similar to the one expected from the *Happism* Theory. The happiness of these communities may not be permanent, but it has been going on for a long time. Also, we can see similar happiness levels in some families embedded in the chaotic surroundings. Such families have been enjoying happiness for a long time now in spite of the multiple violations of *Happism* Considerations going on around them in the society. Such people in these pockets of happiness are very wise and must have followed directly or indirectly *Happism* Considerations. In fact, we can see some small nations today having a very high GNH number which can be almost similar to the one when *Happism* Theory will be perfectly in place. Such happy small nations should remember that the world is getting smaller and smaller. Also, all national economies are entangled into one global economy. Violation of *Happism* Considerations in some nation can affect the happiness in these small happy nations. The point here is: such happiness of small nations is not permanent and sustainable in the absence of *Happism*. On the other hand, the individual happy family surrounded by all the violation conditions of *Happism* Considerations, has already figured out how to be happy no matter what happens around them, except for the forces of the fifth dimension. This brings us to the corollary of the principle that unhappy are those who deserve to be unhappy, except in a case of forces from the fifth dimension. The corollary is: Except for the forces from the fifth dimension, wise and virtuous people are always happy. Pockets of individual happiness can exist and still exist in this world. Similar situations may be seen in primitive communities living in remote jungles.

The above discussion of small nations and an individual family or community living happily in spite of the surrounding chaos is to encourage efforts for personal happiness, no matter what happens in the outside world. But our aim here is global permanent and sustainable happiness which can be achieved only by adopting the *Happism* Theory.

A Nation of Fish Type 3 or Fish Type 4

Even after fully implementing *Happism*, there can be a nation where internal disputes may flair up occasionally. They may be momentary or for a long period of time. Such nation has not fully comprehended god's philosophy. Other nations should not interfere in the affair of such nation, so long as its conflict and its repercussions do not spill outside its border. Let that nation sort out its internal differences. Eventually the warring factions may learn their lessons like Fish Type3 or may never learn like Fish Type 4. It will depend on the wisdom of its political and religious leaders. The leaders from other nations may advise this nation. But, it will be a verbal or written advice and nothing else. Again, one can take the horse to the water but cannot make it drink. Also we reiterate the old principle— unhappy are those who deserve to be unhappy barring the forces from the fifth dimension. However, there is one exceptional situation: Through humanitarian point of view, it is the bounden duty of world nations to actively intervene in a domestic conflict of any nation to end the large scale massacre of its innocent civilians, if the massacre is resulting from that domestic conflict.

The above example of a nation with internal disputes emphasizes the importance of god's philosophy and more so in believing in god, even after full implementation of *Happism* Theory. Remembering or worshipping god often reminds us about the virtues, since god is an embodiment of virtues. That is the reason why we should believe in god's philosophy. Believing in god's philosophy without belief in god lacks the self-cleansing mechanism and may pollute the heart by indulging in sinful activities in due course of time. Nation of Fish Type 4 never realizes the importance of god's philosophy and god's hypothesis.

Happism Impacts on "PASIE" Nations

I am aware that impact of the *Happism* Theory, during the process of implementation and after full execution is different on different nations depending on Population, Area, Scientific progress, Industries, Environment (PASIE), etc. Here we classify different nations based on their current PASIE status. Their classification will be PASIE1, PASIE2, etc. We will discuss the impact on these different PASIE nations during and after the execution of *Happism* Theory.

1. *PASIE1 Nation—Nation with Large Area, Limited Industry and Sparse Population*

    Such a nation generally depends on its export from natural resources or raw industrial goods and does not have enough manpower or even the will to expand its manufacturing base. It is noted here that *Happism* dictates: no nation can increase its manufacturing and production level above its current level. However, it can decrease it depending on its judgment of demand and supply. As the world population goes down during the execution of *Happism* Theory, this nation's exports are reduced but the manufactured goods it imports will be available at cheaper rates, by consideration of demand and supply. Therefore, this type of nation will not be adversely affected economically. Using the formula of Allowable Population Quota this nation may have a scope to increase its population, if it finds it beneficial economically or otherwise, considering the changing needs of the rest of the world during and after the execution of the Theory.

2. *PASIE2 Nation—A Nation with Large Population, Small Industrial Base and Small Land Area*

Such nation is adversely affected by the high population density, relatively small natural resources, and small industrial output resulting in small per capita income. During and after the execution of *Happism* Theory, this type of nation will be benefited in almost all aspects of *Happism* Considerations. Population density will reduce, environmental conditions will be greatly improved, the Green Earth effect will be apparently visible, foreign imports will be available at cheaper rates, per capita income will be higher, etc. In general, the quality of life will be improved considerably. Less population congestion will result in reduction in crime rate, reduction in conflicts among internal factions, etc., adding to the tranquility, peace and the GNH number.

3. *PASIE3 Nation— A Nation with Large Land Area, Medium Population Density and Large Industrial Base*

Such a nation exports large quantities of industrial goods. This export can be reduced because of the reduction in the world population. To start with, the nation may or may not have a scope to reduce its population as per the formula of APQ. But, because of its large industrial base, it may be allowing immigration of qualified personnel from other nations. Such immigration can be stopped. At the same time a pool of qualified citizens can be increased by proper educational system to replace the migrant qualified personnel. To sustain its large industrial base, there may be many research institutes, national labs, etc., working in scientific and industrial fields. This activity will be terminated at the start of the *Happism* implementation. Extra scientific and industrial cadre will be asked to work in ARF areas defined earlier. This will reduce pollution and improve environmental conditions since the manufacturing activity may slow down because of the demand and supply situation. It is further noted here that the reduction in non-ARF and manufacturing activities will not cause any unemployment because this newly available manpower will work on environmental projects such as the beautification of Earth, improve the quality of air and water, increase in acreage of forest land, etc. In fact, there will not be any unemployment because of the reduction in national population and complete stoppage of immigration. The question is: will the per capita income be reduced because of the slowing down of exports? To answer this question, we have to look at the import situation of this nation. Because of the free economy, foreign goods are imported, particularly daily use consumer goods, in large quantities from the countries where manpower is cheap. The nation under study is rich considering per capita income, large natural resources and Gross National Product (GNP). It does not mind to have a negative balance of trade to support its high standard of living. Since the imports are cheap because of the reduction in demand, it is obvious that the net effect will be smaller expenses on daily consumer goods and increase in per capita income and savings. Resulting economic statistic will prove this, if monetary activities are properly supervised by the leading economists of the nation.

4. *PASIE4 Nation—Forest Dwelling Nation*

This nation has learned how to live in harmony with Mother Nature. The outside world should not interfere in the domestic affairs of this nation, unless asked for help in cases of emergencies such as rampant disease, natural disasters, etc. If these people have in place god's philosophy, then they should be very happy in spite of the fact that they are scientifically backward. These people are the good example to show that happiness of a nation depends basically on natural beauty, abundant supply of daily necessity goods as per the requirement of the society (requirement defined by the local people and not by the outsiders) and most of all, our belief in god and god's philosophy. Scientific and technical knowledge can add to the happiness so long as it does not define daily necessity. The situation such as knowledge fomenting necessity and then necessity forcing more and more scientific and technical knowledge and production is detrimental to the happiness of a nation. This situation creates unending artificial needs the satisfaction of which will be like running after a mirage or trying to take a close-up picture of a horizon. In that case human race will end up like a person in the Tolstoy story of "How much land does a man need?"

5. *PASIE5 Nation—Small Land Acreage, Large Population, Highly Industrialized Nation*

This nation is living in a concrete jungle, high rise buildings and factories everywhere. People are under constant pressure of production, performance, and recession. If the population is reduced in half, its industrial output will suffer. Be it that way. Such nations are small in number compared to the rest of the world. Reduction in the industrial output of this nation will not affect much the overall demand and supply situation in the world particularly when the world population will be only half. Quality of life of the citizens of this nation will improve considerably. Since the population reduction is dramatic, there will be no more unemployment, everyone is almost guaranteed of a job, no more concrete jungle, people living in harmony with beautiful nature, etc. With the current scientific and industrial knowledge with fantastic natural beauty, the nation can be almost a paradise. Just a small reminder here, scientific and technical knowledge is neither necessary nor sufficient for a nation to be a paradise.

6. *PASIE6 Nation—Nation with Large Land Acreage, Large Population Density and Small Scientific Base*

Two types of nations can be included in this category: (a) A nation with large land but mostly inhabitable because of the desert, the oil fields, the mountains, etc. Its population is concentrated in a small region. For example, a nation's 95 percent population lives in 4 percent land area, (b) A nation with large habitable land with a very large population. Such nation of type (a) or type (b) will have poor standards of living, overcrowding, damaged environment, occasional religious conflicts, corruption due to the lust for foreign scientific and consumer goods, etc. Religious and political leaders, technocrats, civil servants, and most of the society can be after becoming-quick-rich schemes. Existence of belief in god and god's philosophy is overshadowed by the decadence in the society and nation in general. If we think point by point, it is not hard to conclude that all these ills of PASIE6 nation can be tackled by the successful execution of *Happism* Theory.

It is further noted that *Happism* permanently bans any production of industrial goods above the respective current level of any nation. It also bans any new experimental and testing works in scientific and technical fields, (except ARF areas). Then, is it that the above situation will permanently make some nations dependent on the others for a particular type of goods? The answer is "Yes." But we should remember that the world economy is totally entangled. Every nation is importing some raw material and/or industrial, scientific, and consumer goods. Even today, the human race is smart enough not to start a large scale trade war. When the world population is only half of today's, the probability of a trade war is further reduced. Thus, mutual dependence of world nations is a healthy sign of happy coexistence.

PASIE Nations in Absence of Happism

It is obvious, if the current situation on Planet Earth continues, without the presence of *Happism*; different PASIE nations will have their separate destinies. Here we will speculate what the fate will be of each PASIE nation if *Happism* is not executed.

1. *PASIE1 Nation*

Such a nation has a limited industrial base. It exports raw material but imports large quantities of consumer goods and finished products. In the absence of *Happism*, the world population will continuously increase, and also the demand for consumer goods and finished products. This will increase the import cost of PASIE1 nation, adversely affecting its economy. It is not surprising to see that the percentile increase in the price of exporting raw material or natural goods is much less compared to the percentile increase in the cost of imported consumer goods and finished products. This will reduce the standard of living of PASIE1 nation. It will also create unhappiness and anxiety in the citizens because of the frequently occurring economic fluctuations. Thus, in spite of its large natural resources and small population density, this nation's GNH number will be progressively smaller and smaller in absence of *Happism*.

2. *PASIE2 Nation*

This type of nation has a large population, limited industry, small natural resources, and small land mass. In the absence of *Happism*, the future of this nation is very dark. On almost every front of *Happism* Consideration, this nation is on the slippery slope of national doom. They better sign on *Happism* as early as possible before their miseries get irreversible.

3. *PASIE3 nation*

This nation has a large area, medium population density, and a large industrial base. It has a high standard of living, and large per capita income. It generally has a negative balance of trade i.e. import expenses more than the export value. In absence of *Happism*, it will have more negative balance of trade. Because of the increase in world population, manpower will be cheap and outsourcing will be more and more profitable, unless the efficiency of manpower in such PASIE3 nation is continuously increased. Such an increase may not cope with the exponential increase in world population. This will have two effects: outsourcing will increase, and so will increase unemployment; and secondly, the standard of living of PASIE3 nation will slide toward that of the rest of the world. Another important adverse effect on PASIE3 nation is caused by too many fluctuations in the national economy. This induces tremendous uncertainty in day to day life of citizens, resulting in divorces, crime rates, and many other ills in the society. Even though the life expectancy may improve; the overall quality of mental, physical, and psychological factor will deteriorate. If Environment Consideration improves, its rate of improvement will not be adequate for the betterment of national happiness. These are the major reasons why the GNH number of such a nation is not very high in spite of its large GDP and abundant natural resources compared to its population. It is further noted that PASIE3 nation has already a negative trade balance because of large imports of consumer goods from cheap manpower nations. When *Happism* is not in place, world population will increase exponentially, and so will the demand and price of consumer goods. This will further increase the negative trade balance of PASIE3 nation. In absence of *Happism*, a brilliant brainpower will be wasted in discovering redundant things which will not enhance human happiness. Such a nation should avoid the situation of "what goes up must come down" by adopting the efforts for successful *Happism*. The PASIE3 nation should understand that GNH improvement of all the nations is a key to the success of *Happism* and the permanent happiness of any nation without *Happism* is a myth.

4. *PASIE4 Nation*

This is a forest dwelling nation. If it follows god's philosophy and belief in god; it will continue to enjoy a happy life since it has learned how to live in harmony with nature. In that case, it need not adopt *Happism* to remain happy, so long as other nations do not interfere in its internal affairs. Only exceptional situations, as stated earlier, will be an outside help in case of natural disasters, pandemic diseases, or forces from the fifth dimension in general.

5. *PASIE5 Nation*

The small land, large population, and highly industrialized nation will be greatly affected in the absence of *Happism*. Population will continuously increase causing unbearable congestions, particularly in big cities. Industrial output will be at high gear further ruining the environmental conditions. High population density will cause social problems. Such a nation will not be truly happy unless it reduces its population, no matter what its economic condition will be. The point here is: no nation can be happy without *a* beautiful environment and beautiful nature. With a smaller land area this nation has to reduce its population to live in harmony with nature.

6. *PASIE6 Nation*

This nation has a large land, a high population density, and a small industrial base. The absence of *Happism* will impose unlimited miseries on the citizens. This nation is already on the slippery slope of all the *Happism* Considerations. Implementation of *Happism* is the only way to stop this slide and bring permanent and sustainable happiness for this nation.

Summary of Leadership Duties in Happism

Here is the summary of the work expected from the political, religious, community and-national leaders of every nation for the successful execution of *Happism*:

- The leaders should prepare the mental background of the citizens to adopt the "one woman, one child" principle, till the national population reduces to its APQ level. Thereafter, the population will be held steady at ZPG rate.

- It is extremely important that the citizens learn god's philosophy through religious or other righteous literature for a tolerant and virtuous society. The leaders should see that the citizens understand and implement the principle of "Success and Happiness through Virtues". Belief in god should be emphasized by the leaders to keep society virtuous, away from the sinful means.

- The leaders should see that various "Check Committees" and "Counter-Check Committees" are doing their jobs properly to ensure the successful implementation of all *Happism* Considerations.

Eternal Peace and Heaven on Earth

Here we try to summarize the final effect and influence of on the human race.

1. *Beautiful Planet Earth—Excellent Environment*

   ARF work with added manpower to execute it, reduction in population density, and frozen production levels will guarantee this.

2. *Abundant Leisure to Enjoy Beautiful Planet Earth*

   Happism creates an ideal situation to reduce the burden on the human brain to learn an unnecessary scientific and technical knowledge. It also relieves the pressure of job-related anxieties. Resulting short daily working hours, more vacation days, shortened study years for students, etc., add to the daily and annual leisure hours available to enjoy the beauty of nature. This situation further reminds us that reduction in the standard of living, (if at all it happens), may not have any bearing on the GNH index, since Economic Wellness Factor number 1 will be justifiably given small weightage in the calculation of the GNH number.

3. *Peace on Earth*

   Happism Border Consideration will basically eliminate all the territorial wars between neighboring nations. Religious Consideration demands complete religious tolerance. Every nation can have its own definition of virtues and vices as long as it does not create any problem for other nations. The religious and political leaders will see that belief in god and god's philosophy are properly observed. The citizens and their leaders will decide what political system to follow for the governance of their nation. The religious leaders and the law of land will make sure that people at large properly understand the importance of the doctrine "Success and Happiness through Virtues" as postulated by god's philosophy. If a nation has some shortcomings in executing these ideas resulting in internal conflict, then the nation will end up in a situation based on if it is Fish Type 3 or Fish Type 4. Other nations will not interfere in the internal affairs of such nation. Again, "Unhappy are those who deserve to be unhappy except under the adverse influence of the forces from the fifth dimension". Since Considerations of *Happism* are well defined, it is easy to identify a nation violating them. The rest of the world will jointly force such a nation to follow *Happism*. The resulting international conflict will be short-lived since it is one nation against rest of the world.

4. *No Fluctuations in Economic Health of Nations*

Eventual balance of demand and supply is easy to achieve because of the constant world population at half of the current level. Abundant natural resources will eliminate any situation of a Trade War. Unemployment will be almost nonexistent since the population is only half and manufacturing is frozen to *Happism* starting level or it can even be reduced to balance demand and supply. Also, ARF areas and environment beautification will always absorb extra manpower.

5. *Improved Standard of Living for all Nations*

Reduction in population and frozen production level with due consideration to demand and supply, will improve standard of living for all nations.

If human race sincerely tries to execute *Happism* Considerations, it is easy to create a "Steady State World" at optimum happiness level. World powers and superpowers should realize that discovering how the universe was created and sending a man to Mars is an economic waste and waste of the human brain. It may satisfy their ego but will not add to the happiness of their citizens. The Human race need not go to Mars to find happiness. We can make it happen here on Earth if we channel our efforts in making *Happism* successful. Let us restore the beauty of Mother Earth and live in harmony with nature. Let us "Live and Let Live, Smile and Spread Smile." For that reason, world powers and superpowers should exert their influence in UNO and make the world nations follow *Happism* Considerations in earnest. This is the only way to create heaven on earth and spread permanent and sustainable happiness through eternal peace.

Part 3
Happism: A System Oriented Solution (SOS) for National and International Problems

Happism: A "TOE" of Problem Solver

Physicists are trying to come up with a unique theory called the Theory of Everything (TOE) to explain all the phenomena occurring in our universe. The Theory of *Happism* was originally devised to spread "Permanent and Sustainable Happiness on Planet Earth". If adopted by the world nations, the theory has a potential to create Heaven on Earth through eternal peace. *Happism* is a natural and rational outcome of the discourse on "Success and Happiness" given in Part 1 earlier. Since the base of the theory is a perfect rationale, there is no intrinsic buildup of any bias towards any faction such as: the conservative or the liberal, the rich or the poor, religion "A" or religion "B", skin color "C" or skin color "D", the developed nation or the developing nation, etc. As a result, any *Happism* solution of a national or an international problem should be acceptable to all the world nations.

The seven "Considerations" of Part 2, "Manifesto of *Happism*", are like a computer algorithm in which the input is a definition of any national or international problem and the corresponding output being its rational solution. This is possible because, the seven Considerations were postulated accounting for the happiness of humanity through all the 360 degree angles. If we think about the corollary of this situation, any problematic case facing a nation or a group of nations should have an algorithm of solution coded in these seven Considerations. Based on the problem definition, appropriate Weightage Factor (WF) can be allocated to each Consideration. This will result in a perfect System Oriented Solution (SOS) for any global riddle. Thus, *Happism* will be a TOE for human race to solve its national or international problems.

The seven Considerations of *Happism* Manifesto are summarized in the next section. The detailed explanation can be reviewed in Part 2 given earlier. This Manifesto is repeated here to make Part 3 a self-explanatory session.

Manifesto of Happism

The People and the leaders of each and every nation must take an oath to uphold the following Considerations.

1. *Population Consideration*:

Every nation is allocated its Allowable Population Quota (APQ), which is the larger of the following (a) and (b) numbers.

Allowable Population Quota = Half of the current population of the nation, Allowable Population Quota = (Total square mile area of the nation) X 10, i.e. maximum allowable population density is 10 per square mile

Every country must enforce the rule of "One woman one child" till it trims down its population to its APQ level. Once the population reaches APQ the rate of child birth will be permanently locked at Zero Population Growth (ZPG) rate. Note that, if a nation chooses, its population can be below APQ, but never more. Also, if the nation chooses, immigration is allowed subjected to the condition that total population does not exceed APQ.

2. *Border Consideration*:

Borders of all the nations are frozen permanently to the current state.

3. *Weapon Consideration*:

The weapon arsenal of any nation is frozen to its current level. No nation is allowed to develop any new weapon system nor allowed to increase the quantity of weapons it possesses already. Weapon production is limited to the level required for internal law and order usage. Exporting of the weapons is allowed, subjected to the condition that weapon importing nation uses it strictly for establishing its internal law and order situation and not for any foreign aggression.

4. *Science and Technology Research Consideration:*

All the research work on science and technology will be permanently stopped except in the areas of Allowable Research Field (ARF), such as medicine, pharmacy, agriculture, horticulture, Global Warming and Green Earth. Current technical and scientific knowledge of the human race is enough to keep it happy, particularly when its population is only half. Extra knowledge is redundant and waste of money and manpower. Savings in these fields should be diverted to the areas of ARF. Thus, the scientific and technical knowledge is frozen to the respective current level of that nation. The nation may improve its theoretical knowledge to the maximum current level human race has attained. But the experimental and testing works are permanently banned except in ARF areas.

5. *Production Consideration:*

The manufacturing capacity, production level and acquisition of raw materials are frozen to the respective current states of a give nation. Based on demand and supply, the nation may reduce but never surpass these respective current states. Also, there will be unrestricted imports and exports of raw materials and manufactured goods between world nations. This implies that if some country wants advanced scientific gadgetry it can import it rather than trying to develop it on its own. By this arrangement the country will spare its population from learning any practical application of scientific and technical knowledge more than what it knows currently.

6. *Religious Consideration:*

All religions and their leaders must respect and be tolerant of other religions. There will be a complete freedom for an individual to follow any religion that greatly emphasizes virtues and nothing but virtues. No attempt of religious conversions is permitted. God's philosophy of success and happiness through virtues will be vigorously, judiciously, and constantly followed.

7. *Environmental Consideration:*

Every nation and its leaders must improve its environment such as quality of air and water, acreage of forest land, etc. It should not be a big task as the population is only half, production is reduced, and a large number of scientists and technocrats are working toward agriculture, horticulture and Green Earth research of ARF areas.

If a country refuses to follow these considerations then that country will cease to exist. It will be divided into surrounding countries based on the lengths of common borders. An island nation will be absorbed in its nearest country. This task will be carried out by the rest of the world nations working together. Since this conflict will be one rogue nation against rest of the world, it will be an easy and a short-lived task. It is further noted here that to be permanently and sustainably happy, the steps to be followed by all the nations, rich or poor, are the same. I am very optimistic. There is nothing impossible for the human race. It can easily adopt these considerations and bring permanent and sustainable happiness on Earth.

Principle Pillars of Happism

SOS is based on the seven considerations of the *Happism* Manifesto. The latter in its turn, is derived from the principles essential for success and happiness in the life of an individual or of a nation in general. Thus, the roots of SOS are indirectly embedded in these principles. If a certain SOS of a national or an international problem is objected by some faction, then the principle over which the objectionable part is based can be revisited to evaluate its rationality and applicability in context of the objection.

The relevant principles with their designated numbers are listed here for ease in referencing them during the subsequent SOS discussions.

Principle 1: By the strength of your military, you may conquer the country, but you cannot convert its people to your political or religious system. You can take the horse to the water forcefully. That's all you can do.

Principle 2: The situation, the religious leaders are supposed to enhance the moral standard of the nation but they are not politically powerful, can be resolved only by electing wise and virtuous political leaders who have already acquired high moral standards under the coaching of the religious leaders.

Principle 3: It is imperative that all the nations should adopt uniform moral standards and definitions of those critical virtues and critical vices which have a potential to affect the happiness of other nations. This will eliminate the gap between mass mentality and individual thinking. Then only the lasting peace and happiness will prevail. It is a falsehood to think that since all the countries are happy, peace will prevail in the world. The world will be sitting on the time bomb of conflict between moral standards and nonuniform definitions of critical virtues and vices.

Principle 4: In the olden days, the king used to mold his citizenry. Nowadays, "Time" evolves society and the society selects its leader. This line of thinking very easily helps me to conclude that "Time" creates exceptional personalities and not the other way round. "Time" rules supreme and not the human being.

Principle 5: Opportune "Time" can create historic personalities like Lincoln, Gandhi, Churchill, etc. We should just try sincerely to execute *Happism*. "Time" will create

Lincolns, Gandhis, and Churchills, if we give "Time" a chance by our own efforts.

Principle 6: Religion is not the only means to create a virtuous population. Law and order can force people to follow the virtuous or legal path. But virtues are something within, that is intrinsic to a person. Law and order is something thrust on the society. Once the grip of law is released, the person or the society in general may tend to practice illegal means full of vices.

Principle 7: The root cause of suffering, miseries, and unhappiness in any community is the lack of proper leadership.

Principle 8: Violating number 3, Weapon Consideration, results in creating an endless chain reaction of weapon competition, particularly the spread of nuclear weapons. In that case a brute force is justified as a last resort against the nation sponsoring such nuclear proliferation.

Principle 9: Other nations should not interfere in the internal affairs of any nation, as long as its domestic conflict and its repercussions do not spill outside its border. Let that nation sort out its internal differences. Eventually the warring factions may learn their lessons like Fish Type 3 or may never learn like Fish Type 4. However, there is one exceptional situation: Through humanitarian point of view, it is the bounden duty of world nations to actively intervene in a domestic conflict of any nation to end the large scale massacre of its innocent civilians, if the massacre is resulting from that domestic conflict.

Principle 10: There is no doubt that the human race and its uncontrolled population growth, along with rampant manufacturing plants to satisfy the insatiable thirst of material goods, have ruined our environment. Scientific and technical knowledge can add to the happiness so long as it does not define daily necessity. The situation such as a knowledge fomenting necessity and then necessity forcing more and more scientific and technical knowledge and production is detrimental to the happiness of a nation. This situation creates an unending artificial need, the satisfaction of which will be like running after a mirage, or trying to take a close-up picture of a horizon. In that case the human race will end-up like a person in the Tolstoy story of "How Much Land Does a Man Need?"

Principle 11: World powers and superpowers should realize that discovering how the universe was created and sending a man to Mars is an economic waste and a waste of the human brain. It may satisfy their egos but this will not add to the happiness of their citizens.

Principle 12: Snap-Shot of Shangri-La Society— Please refer to Part 1, Section "Paradigm Shift in GNH Weightage Factors".

Principle 13: Virtues can breed success in life, and success in life obtained through virtues can make one happy. God's Philosophy gives us success and happiness through virtues. Worshipping god constantly or even intermittently reminds us to be virtuous and stay virtuous.

Principle 14: Unhappy are those who deserve to be unhappy, barring the forces from the fifth dimension (forces beyond one's control).

Principle 15: To be successful in life, one need not be virtuous. But to be happy, one must achieve success through virtues.

Principle 16: If everyone surrounding you is immoral then to be immoral becomes the norm of the society. Definitions of virtues and vices are reversed. The connection between success and happiness carried by virtuous particles only, collapses.

Principle 17: Religion by itself cannot make you happy, unless you have proper wisdom. Following the righteous path of religion along with your wisdom can lead you to eternal bliss. If many of us choose to follow the path of a jihadist to acquire our eternal bliss, what type of world will we be living in?— A world of dumb people massacring one another?

Principle 18: Religious leaders are those who teach their followers to be successful and happy through virtues. This is the God's Philosophy they believe and practice.

Principle 19: Happiness is tied with wisdom and virtues and not with the wealth. Up to a certain limit of poverty, wealth has little influence on individual happiness.

Principle 20: All the religions aim at making followers virtuous. But the problem comes in interpreting the religious scripts.

Principle 21: As Abraham Lincoln has said, "You cannot enrich the poor by pooring the rich". Here we have ruined the happiness of downstream people to enrich the happiness of the upstream ones. That is against what Lincoln has stated and what *Happism* expects. The measure should uplift the happiness of all and not of one at the cost of the other.

Principle 22: It is possible to formulate a fundamental law of nature governing an apparently chaotic phenomenon in universe.

Principle 23: Appropriate wiring of brain circuitry depicted in the horoscope, which also represents the destiny factor, is a necessary but not a sufficient condition to achieve Einstein-type greatness. Even though one may not believe in Astrology, the conclusions drawn from it are true for all the circumstances.

Principles 24: Success in life is measured with respect to certain datum level defined by the heritage of a person.

Principle 25: The story of Four Fish—

Fish Type 1: Born Great,
Fish Type 2: Learns from
Other's Mistakes,
Fish Type 3: Learns by One's
Own Mistakes,
Fish Type 4: Commits Same Mistakes
Repeatedly, and Never
Learns, but Suffers
Life Long.

Principle 26: Live and Let Live, Smile and Spread Smile.

Principle 27: Some say: Life is that as you take it. For me: Life is that as you make it.

Principle 28: Know Thyself.

Principle 29: No one says that life is a bed of roses. But with smart efforts, one gets better and better in throwing away the thorns and leaving the pure roses behind to enjoy.

Principle 30: Brute force is justified as a last resort against a nation which refuses to join the successful execution of *Happism*.

SOS Format for National and International Problems

The format of System Oriented Solution (SOS) is exactly the same for all the problems. Weightage Factor (WF) of a given *Happism* Consideration will be zero or equal to all other nonzero WFs. The zero WF indicates: That the Consideration has no influence on the outcome of the problem under study. The procedure of variable WFs is a unique problem-dependent situation. Its details are explained in Part 2, section "Revised Definition of GNH Number". However, the nonzero WFs will have mostly the same value, signifying that all Considerations are equally important to arrive at the correct SOS for the problem under study.

It is further noted that SOS gives a general solution outline of the problem-free ground that covers different areas such as national defense, internal law and order, foreign affairs, scientific progress to "keep-up with Joneses", human happiness derived from God's Philosophy, democratic principles, clean environment, etc. The actual implementation of SOS to cover any individual area is basically left to its corresponding experts.

The suggested format of SOS is as follows:

A. Problem Definition

This section gives a summary narration of the history and also the current status of the problem.

B. SOS Based on *Happism* Considerations

This section explains: How to apply the seven *Happism* Manifesto Considerations to solve the national or the international problem under study. In some special, nonobvious cases, proper numbers of *Happism* Principles are cited to support the rationale behind the proposed solution.

1. Population Consideration: WF1
Description of SOS derived from this Consideration.

2. Border Consideration: WF2
Description of SOS derived from this Consideration.

3. Weapon Consideration:WF3
Description of SOS derived from this Consideration.

4. Science and Technology Research Consideration: WF4
Description of SOS derived from this Consideration.

5. Production Consideration: WF5
Description of SOS derived from this Consideration.

6. Religious Consideration: WF6
Description of SOS derived from
this Consideration.

7. Environmental Consideration:WF7
Description of SOS derived from
this Consideration.

C. Discussion of Ideal Solution and
Nonideal Eventualities:

During the discussion of Nonideal
Eventualities, the cited principle will be
reevaluated for its applicability and reasoning.
Any controversy leading to the nonideal solution
will be addressed to the satisfaction of the party
objecting to the Ideal Solution generated in
Section B. As mentioned earlier, since SOS is
unbiased, no one should have any objection to
the result. But in case, rational discussion of the
principle used for the objectionable part will
help to die-down the controversy.

1. Nonideal Eventuality 1
Describe pros and cons of nonideal solution.
2. Nonideal Eventuality 2
Describe pros and cons of nonideal solution.
ETC.

The subsequent sections here are devoted
to produce rational solution outlines for the
typical national and/or international problems
currently haunting the world philosophers,
thinkers and leaders in general. In every case,
problem definition is an input to the above

SOS Format and the corresponding output is the required solution based on the *Happism* Theory Principles.

Civil War in Syria

(Note: When this solution was suggested, Assad's opposition was united to fight for democracy. The subsequent tern of events has proved the validity of this SOS).

A. Problem Definition:

This is a typical case of a dictator who has lost the support of majority of his citizens. President Bashar al-Assad supported by Baath Party has a support of 15 percent of the population. He has all the military might at his disposal and he is using it to massacre the opposition, resulting in widespread civilian casualties. The current figure of dead is more than 60,000 and it is ongoing. The opposition consists of the volunteer civilians and the soldiers who left Assad regime. Their aim is to end the state of emergency, remove Assad and his cronies, establish democratic freedom, etc. Since the opposition is receiving military aid from many foreign countries, Assad regime has dubbed it as insurgents of armed terrorists and foreign mercenaries.

B. SOS Based on *Happism* Considerations:

Here, we come up with the solution based on the principles of *Happism* theory and it's

Manifesto. The current situation clearly shows: Assad government is grossly in violation of God's Philosophy of Manifesto number 6, Religious Considerations referred in Part 2. This violation is responsible for more than 60,000 deaths. As mentioned in the last paragraph of the Manifesto, also as stated in the section titled "Justification of Brute Force" of Part 2, it is recommended here that other nations should jointly remove Assad government and help to establish democratic rule. Once this is achieved, the role of other nations is over. Let the Syrian people prove if they are Fish Type 3 or Fish Type 4 (Principles 9 and 25).

When the Syrian people are bestowed with democratic power, they should follow Manifesto Considerations as specified here, to avoid repetition or recurrence of the current problem of civil war.

1. Population Consideration: WF1=0

    This Consideration has no bearing on the current problem.

2. Border consideration: WF2 not equal to 0

    The democratically elected government must make the national borders impervious to out-of-country miscreants trying to enter Syria.

3. Weapon Consideration: WF3 not equal to 0

    The country should be adequately armed for self defense and internal law and order.

4. Science and Technology Research
   Consideration: WF4 not equal to 0

    In the current situation, since other nations continue this research work, Syria is also entitled to do so.

5. Production Consideration: WF5 not
   equal to 0

    In the current situation, since other nations continue their production, Syria is also entitled to do so.

6. Religious Consideration: WF6 not equal to 0

    The democratically elected government must follow God's Philosophy and Belief, (Principles 13 through 20). Also Principles 1 through 12 should be judiciously followed, where ever applicable.

7. Environmental Consideration: WF7 = 0

    Not applicable to the current Civil War problem.

C. Discussion of Ideal Solution and Nonideal Eventualities:

    The ideal solution of establishing the democratic government in Syria with the help of other nations (Principle 9) is discussed above. This ideal scenario can be threatened by the external mercenaries already in Syria and also by the internal factions amongst Syrian people themselves. People may elect nontolerant, ultraconservative religious leaders oppressing minorities and women. This will be their internal problem. Let them sort it out without any interference from outside nations unless there is another large scale massacre. Here the following two *Happism* principles are applicable; Principle 14 for Syrian people, Principle 1 for the rest of world nations. Principle 14 says: Unhappy are those who deserve to be unhappy, barring the forces from the fifth dimension (forces beyond one's control). Principle 1 states: By the strength of your military, you may conquer the country, but you cannot convert its people to your political or religious system. You can take the horse to the water forcefully. That's all you can do.

Gun Homicide Rate in USA

A. Problem Definition:

More than 11,000 people were killed in gun-related violence during the year 2011. It is mind-boggling to read the statistics given in a *Time Magazine* issue of January 14, 2013. The number of firearms is almost the same as the number of men, women and children in the USA (88.8 per 100 people). Gun homicide rate of USA (3.2 per 100,000 people) is by far the highest among the developed nations, in fact 6.4 times higher than the nearest second (Norway 0.5 per 100,000), and 32 times higher than the third highest Canada and Australia. These murders in the USA included mass killings of innocent people and personal or gang-related violence. Growth of firearm manufacturing has sky-rocketed between the year 2001 and 2011 as reported by the official government site atf.gov/statistics. About 95 percent of these firearms are used in USA.

B. SOS Based on *Happism* Considerations:

This System Oriented Solution is a classic case of how *Happism* Theory tackles the national problems through 360 degree angles. The relevant *Happism* Considerations are now applied one by one for this gun violence problem in USA.

1. Population Consideration: WF1=0
   Not relevant to this problem.

2. Border Consideration: WF2 not equal to 0
   National borders should be firmly secured so that the drugs, drug lords and their gangs cannot enter the USA. This is to avoid any addition to the current grim statistics.

3. Weapon Consideration: WF3 not equal to 0
   The most moral and ethical urgency is to stop mass killings of innocent people. If any person needs some explanations for this then he/she should be sent to Siberia to understand the importance of saving an innocent life! Anyway, there should be an immediate ban on assault weapons and high-capacity ammunition clips or magazines which are extensively used in the mass killings

of innocent people. Each adult (age 21 years and above) will be allowed one pistol and one hunting rifle, each with non-rapid firing mechanism holding ten bullets maximum. An appropriate gun buyback program should be introduced by the federal or state or local city government.

4. Science and Technology Research Consideration: WF4 not equal to 0

In the current situation, since other nations continue this research, USA is also entitled to do so. Special emphasis should be given to the mental and psychological aspect of Allowable Research Field (ARF). Also, a research work is needed to understand a connection, if any, between violent video games and gun violence. No ban on these games is recommended till this correlation is established.

5. Production Consideration: WF5 not equal to 0

Production of assault weapons and high capacity ammunition clips is for the military usage only. Pistol and hunting rifle along with their ammunition should be produced as per the above requirement of Weapon Consideration.

6. Religious Consideration: WF not equal to 0

Principles 13 through 20 should be vigorously, judiciously and constantly followed by all the citizens. As stated in Principle 6, proper law and order should also be enforced to make people follow the virtuous and legal path.

Almost all the gang related murders occur in the society of "Forgotten" defined in Part 1, section "Social Obligations towards Downtrodden and Forgotten". Therefore, the recommendations of that section should be followed to reduce the gang-related homicide rate in USA.

It is a bound duty of a gun seller to check that he/she is not selling the gun to a misfit such as a mentally ill or an underage or a criminal person. The government agency ATF and the shop owners should maintain relevant Records of the Misfits (ROM). Proper background check should be in place at all the times for all the buyers. Medical professionals should make sure that the names of dangerous mental patients are included in ROM.

7. Environmental Consideration: WF=0

This Consideration has no bearing on the current problem.

C. Discussion of Ideal Solution and Nonideal Eventualities:

Let us go somewhat in details of System Oriented Solution derived here from *Happism* Theory. The implied information of SOS is highlighted in the following discussion:

The gun homicides in USA are divided into two categories:

Category 1: Mass killings of innocent people,
Category 2: Murders due to personal vendetta and gang violence.

Category 1 deaths are about 10 percent to 15 percent of the overall number depending on how one defines "Mass killings". Category 2 deaths are remaining 85 percent to 90 percent. If we define "Devastation Impact Number" (DIN) as a number of people devastated by any murder, then DIN of Category 1 is way higher compared to that of Category 2. Psychological devastation caused in the society is proportional to the DIN value. Broadly speaking, Category 1 murder hurts the feelings of millions of people; whereas, Category 2 death is mourned by say ten immediate family members and friends. So, an average DIN of Category 1 is 12.5 millions and of Category 2 is 87.5 X 10 = 875. Apart from Category1's high DIN number, it is an absolute responsibility of the society or the country to prevent the massacres of innocent people.

The firearm ban proposed in SOS basically affects Category 1 murders. Since the overall death number of this category is small compared to that of Category 2, the gun lobbyists are justified to some extent to say that the proposed ban of firearms will not reduce the gun homicide rate in USA. But they are conveniently ignoring DIN factor as well as the moral and ethical duty of the society to protect innocent people which can be accomplished by the proposed ban.

People involved in the gang wars are basically the "Downtrodden" and the "Forgotten" defined in Part 1; section "Social Obligation towards the Downtrodden and the Forgotten", which details how to create peace and tranquility in this volatile population of the society. Principle 6 of enforced law and order, also Principle 14 regarding personal responsibility are worthy of special mention here. Importance of God's Philosophy and its principles cannot be overemphasized to reduce Category 2 homicide rate in the USA. Also, extra police petrol is recommended in the high crime areas to enforce law and order among Forgotten (Principle 6).

An alternate solution is proposed by some gun lobbyists: not to ban any firearm but to arm every school teacher; also to place armed guards at every school and public place such as movie theatre, shopping mall, library, etc. I agree to this suggestion to the limit of placing one armed guard per busy public place and school. It will be mainly a psychological deterrent to a mass killer, but its practical utility is almost nil. Placing more than one guard is uneconomical and more so, not of much added efficacy. Banning of firearms mentioned in the above Section B is of prime importance to stop the massacres of innocent people.

Some lobbyists point at year 1791 Second Amendment of Constitution: "A well regulated militia, being necessary to the security of a free state, the right of the people to keep and bear Arms, shall not be infringed". In 2008 and 2010 the Court ruled that Second Amendment protects an individual's right to possess a firearm without any connection to militia service. Also, the Court cited some prohibitions and restrictions on firearm possession as constitutional through this Second Amendment. Based on this constitutional information, the gun lobbyists try to justify bearing all types of firearms without any legal restriction. The gun lobbyists should remember that in the current context "The means don't justify the end, the end justifies the means". At the end of the barrel is the life of an innocent person. The current massacres going on in the USA surely justify an adequate ban on some firearms.

A few cunning lobbyists resort to the catchy slogans to attract blind followers. The following two are such examples.

Slogan 1: If we outlaw the guns, only the outlaws will have the guns!

Slogan 2: Guns don't kill people, people kill people!

Part 1; section "Just Do It", gives full explanation to expose the hollow nature of Slogan 1. Slogan 2 is too silly an example of a low-grade propaganda and needs no explanation to refute it.

As a short summary: In the land of the USA, we are trying to sow the seeds of *Happism* Principles by means of System Oriented Solution (SOS). Considering the complex nature of the problem, this seed-sowing process may need multiple modifications and mid-course corrections to attain perfection. Eventually, the good seeds of *Happism* Principles are bound to produce a rich harvest of peace by reducing the gun homicide rate (Principle 29). Any compromise in the quality of seeds will result in expansion of the killing fields in the USA.

Global Warming

A. Problem Definition:

This is a true global phenomenon affecting all the nations. It reveals itself in various forms such as: wild fluctuations in world weather pattern, melting of polar ice caps, tornados, flooding, rising sea levels, extensive crop failures, delayed monsoon rains, disappearance of coral reef formation, etc. The major culprits to cause this phenomenon are: emission of carbon dioxide from cars, coal burning, airplanes, rockets, etc; emission of methane gas from agriculture products and animals; deforestation for farming, wood products, etc.

B. SOS Based on *Happism* Considerations:

It will be seen here that the above causes and their effects of Global Warming are fully addressed by the seven Considerations of *Happism* Theory and its principles.

1. Population Consideration: WF not equal to 0
Here we divide the world nations in two categories: A nation that actually produces harmful emission gases on its land to manufacture some end product, and secondly, the nation that uses this end product. Both these nations should reduce their respective population to pre-empt the use of the end product.

2. Border Consideration: WF2=0
This Consideration has no effect on Global Warming.

3. Weapon Consideration: WF3=0
This Consideration has no effect on Global Warming.

4. Science and Technology Research Consideration: WF4 not equal to 0
Global Warming research comes under Allowable Research Field (ARF), as such be given high priority compared to other scientific and technical areas. This should be reflected in money and manpower allocated to Global Warming research work. Principle 10 is important to reverse Global Warming effects. Principle 11 suggests stopping the devastation

of the Ozone layer and the stratosphere shield caused by polar and upper-stage rockets.

5. Production Consideration: WF5 not equal to 0

Reduction in population will warrant reduction in production and therefore in emission gases causing Global Warming.

6. Religious Consideration: WF6 not equal to 0

Using Principle 6, proper emission laws will be strictly enforced.

7. Environmental Consideration: WF7 not equal to 0

Expansion of rain forests and other Green Earth projects should be given high priorities.

C. Discussion of Ideal Solution and Nonideal Eventualities:

The above *Happism* Considerations, where ever applicable, should be followed by both: emission producing as well as the corresponding manufactured product-using nations. In the absence of proper compliance, the current Global Warming miseries of the human race will multiply exponentially year after year. For example, in some areas during the previous thirty years, monsoon rains have been delayed by three to four weeks. The annual rainfall has decreased by 30 percent to 35 percent. If this pattern continues, there will be no time left to produce even a single drop of monsoon rain. Also, it is needless to remind the havoc played by the cyclones like Katrina and Sandy in a recent past.

Some people do not believe in the global warming phenomenon. They consider it as a hoax. Whatever is happening currently they attribute to the natural changes in global weather pattern. There is no gimmick here to convert the nonbelievers into the believers. But, considering the devastation experienced by the human race every year, it is better to err on the safe side, which is to do something about global warming instead of ignoring it completely.

Palestine Problem

A. Problem Definition:

First and foremost, every nation now has to recognize the fact of life: The state of Israel will exist at its current location for a foreseeable future. The question is: how this existence will be peaceful to Israel, Palestine, and the other nations involved in this conflict? A major thrust of the following SOS is to answer this question morally, ethically, and practically through 360 degree angles.

SOS suggested here considers the well known historical facts. In the year 1947, under the Zionist Movement 700,000 Palestinians were driven out or fled for the fear of their lives from their homes. They were never allowed to return. In May 1948, a Jewish state of Israel was formed. In June of 1948, more Palestinians (350,000) fled or were expelled from the Israel conquered area. In the past sixty five years, many wars were fought between the Arabs and the Israelis. As a result, the current map of Israel came into existence. Palestinians became refugees in the surrounding countries like Syria, Jordan, Lebanon, etc. Recently, a limited statehood was granted to Palestine, which includes West Bank, Gaza Strip and East Jerusalem, the territories captured by Israel in the 1967 Mideast war. The United Nation General Assembly voted overwhelmingly to grant "Nonmember Observer State" status to Palestine. As a result, Palestine State can now approach the UNO bodies such as Criminal Court to seek injustice against war crimes and Israel's action of building settlements on war-won land. July 2009 statistics shows: 305,000 Israelis lived in 121 settlements in the West Bank area. These numbers may have gone up significantly by January 2013.

B. SOS Based on *Happism* Considerations:

The practical solution given here may have some minor difficulties which can be surmounted by the Palestinians with their friendly Arab nations. The following is the outline of SOS obtained from each Consideration:

1. Population Consideration: WF1=0

This Consideration has no bearing on the current problem.

2. Border Consideration: WF2 not equal to 0

The UNO bestowed Palestine State should secure its borders and make them impervious to nonvisa members. The current situation of Palestinians going to Israel territory for jobs and to earn livelihood should be stopped as early as possible, so that they are not dependent on Israel by any means. The current no approach road situation of Gaza Strip should be peacefully negotiated with Israel. Israel has enough territory and should gracefully vacate all the settlements built in UNO-granted Palestine State. If not, the latter can go to UNO Court to enforce it.

3. Weapon Consideration: WF3 not equal to 0

Palestinians should try to be self-sufficient through weapons point of view to guard their borders from external aggression; also to establish law and order in the state. These weapons should not be used to attack any foreign nation, unless being attacked.

4. Science and Technology Research Consideration: WF4 not equal to 0

The Palestinians should give a special emphasis on science, technology and general education of their population.

5. Production Consideration: WF5 not equal to 0

The state should satisfy its daily needs and defense requirements by maintaining the adequate production level.

6. Religious Consideration: WF6 not equal to 0

The population should be tolerant to all the religions and their different sects. The religious and the political leaders should be responsible to establish this situation. Principles 2 through 20 should be vigorously, judiciously and constantly followed.

7. Environmental Consideration: WF7=0

This Consideration is given less priority compared to the enormous task of implementing other Considerations.

C. Discussion of Ideal Solution and Nonideal Eventualities:

The major obstruction to implement above SOS may come from not recognizing Israel's right to exist or continuously trying to attack Israel's territory. Such attacks may come from the radicals or those who cannot digest the reality of life. Palestinians should eradicate from their land all the terrorists' acts going on against Israel. They should honestly and sincerely follow Principle 26: Live and Let Live, Smile and Spread Smile.

In this formative period, the Arab nations should help Palestine State very generously. Also, they should grant full citizenship to the Palestinian refugees who have settled in these

Arab nations before the Syrian War. In fact, for their peace and tranquility the Mideast nations, including Israel, need to follow Principles 1 through 30. Otherwise, the whole region will be permanently "Sick like Fish Type 4", (Principle 25).

(Please refer Appendix 1 for the implementation of this SOS)

Taliban and al-Qaeda in Afghanistan

A. Problem Definition:

These are the people misguided by their religious and political leaders (Principle 20). They believe in Jihad (Principle 17) and spread violence to the rest of the world. They treat their women as slaves. It is a historical fact that as long as the Hindu Kush and the Pamir mountains are there; these people will be living in tribes, speak the language of force and never be civilized.

B. SOS Based on *Happism* Considerations:

Basically, the Taliban and al-Qaeda jihadists are cancer to the human race. There is no cure to this disease. The only thing the rest of the world can do is to confine it to its limited area near the Hindu Kush and Pamir mountain ranges in Afghanistan. Any new cancerous cell outside this area should be eliminated by a surgical operation of laser-guided missiles and other aerial procedures. It is neither necessary nor fruitful to send ground troops in the mountain ranges to chase these people. Confinement is the only correct strategy to deal with them.

In short, the situation boils down to the fact that these people cannot be civilized nor can they uplift themselves to be worthy of world citizens. Therefore, rest of the world nations, instead of trying to humanize them, use the following *Happism* Principles to steer clear of their nuisance:

Principle 7: In this jihadist society, people meet violent deaths, ladies suffer, etc. The root cause, as this principle suggests, is lack of proper leadership.

Principles 9 and 30: These principles are very aptly applicable to the current situation. The Taliban and al-Qaeda people should be left to their own fate so long they do not play any mischief outside their territory (Principle 9). If they do, they should be heavily punished. (Principle 30).

Principles 14 and 20: Crooked interpretation of holy book by their religious leaders cannot be corrected by any other human being. Leave these people alone to their own destiny.

Principle 16: Every person joining Taliban or al-Qaeda is "immoral" as mentioned in this principle.

Principle 17: These people believe in jihad for their Eternal Bliss.

Principle 25: These are Fish Type 4 people, will never learn but repeat the same mistakes again and again.

Principle 26: These people do not believe in the principle of "Live and Let Live, Smile and Spread Smile". They even ban all types of music!

C. Discussion of Ideal Solution and Nonideal Eventualities:

There is no solution to this menace but certain principles to face it, as listed above.

Problems in India
Air Pollution, Water Shortage, Power Shortage, Corruption, Law and Order

A. Problem Definition:

This land of brilliant ancient culture and tolerant people is going through a tremendous turmoil. There is some progress in recent years, but the so called progress revealed by the increase in middle class number (currently about 30 percent of the population) is a sort of hollow progress. Some people who are pulled into the middle class do not earn their middle class status. It is bestowed on them by the government with political intentions. The nation does not get any return from the middle class salary paid to this undeserving section of the middle class.

Population explosion is a ticking time bomb with no immediate fuse to unlock. Various religious factions do not trust one another; as a result, no one is ready to undertake the family planning scheme. All these different shortages are the direct catastrophes from this situation. The whole country has become one hollow tree, eaten up by the termites of corruption. They have crawled in all the branches of social and political lives (Principle 16). Their presence is as clear as a day-light and needs no proof for its existence. Nevertheless, as a formality, here are a few examples involving the politicians and their official cronies:

(a) 1987, Bofors Gun Kickbacks,
(b) 2001, Enron Dabhol Power Plant Scam,
(c) 2010, Commonwealth Games Mega-scandals,
(d) 2011, Adarsh Housing Society Corruption,
(e) 2011, 2G Spectrum Embezzlement,
(f) 2013, Fodder Case Embezzlement.

Each of these corruption cases is of the magnitude similar to Watergate Scandal of USA. And yet, how many of these corrupt politicians and officials have paid for their sins? ———Almost nil!

The quota system is based on the caste and not on the family income. The so-called lower caste people have now moved up in the government jobs and also in the political hierarchy. They are employed at all levels, given easy access to education institutes and are fitted at high posts in all walks of life. Of course, some of them deserve their posts, but many of them are there because of the politically-motivated quota system. These so called lower caste people think that they have suffered enough in the past and the current situation is the passport to good life by all means. So, the corruption is rampant from top to bottom. I do not intend to say that all the lower class people are corrupt and that the lower class people are the only corrupt people. Almost everyone is corrupt, of course, with a few respectable, noble, and moral exceptions

Corruption in the internal security system and judiciary has made it almost impossible to implement any law, which is only a paper tiger now. Some civil law suits are going on for ten, fifteen, twenty years with no end in sight. The Law Minister (Secretary) Mr. Ashwini Kumar has reported in the Indian Parliament that till year 2013 over thirty million cases are pending in various courts. The cadre of political leadership is very pathetic because the population that elects it is narrow minded (Principle 4). As a result, Indian politics is now like a dirty pond where a big fish grows bigger and bigger by swallowing a small fish, and the smallest fish barely survives on the crumbs deliberately dropped by the big fish as a bribe or a bet for electoral votes.

Political dynasties have mushroomed all over and the democracy is nothing but anarchy. As the population increases exponentially, so does the mass scale decadence of the nation. The general public and its leaders should realize this state of the nation. After all, you get what you deserve, Principle 14: Unhappy are those who deserve to be unhappy, barring the forces from the fifth dimension.

The current situation warrants a proper attention at each and every *Happism* Consideration outlined in the next section of the System Oriented Solution.

B. SOS Based on *Happism* Considerations:

1. Population Consideration: WF1 not equal to 0

    The religious and political leaders should come up with a family planning scheme to reduce the population of each religion by the same percentile year after year. There should be proper Check and Counter-Check Committees in place as mentioned in Part 2, section "Obstructions in *Happism* Theory Implementation".

2. Border Consideration: WF2 not equal to 0

    India should seal its borders from the terrorists and other illegal people of adjacent countries. Illegal immigrants currently settled in India should be deported soon.

3. Weapon consideration: WF3 not equal to 0

Adequate arsenal should be available to establish internal law and order, also, to tackle the external aggregation.

4. Science and Technology Research Consideration: WF4 not equal to 0

Since the surrounding countries are engaged in such research activities, India has no choice but to follow suit.

5. Production Consideration: WF5 not equal to 0

Production should be hauled to its peak since all the surrounding nations are trying to do so.

6. Religious Consideration: WF6 not equal to 0

God's Philosophy of "Success and Happiness through Virtues" (Principle 18) should be emblematized and practiced by all. Principles13 through 20 should be clearly understood and executed accordingly.

7. Environmental Consideration: WF7 not equal to 0

Proper air pollution and water pollution laws should be in place and judiciously executed. Research in ARF areas should be given high priority. Principle 6 should be strictly followed to enforce these pollution-related laws.

C. Discussion of Ideal Solution and Nonideal Eventualities:

Honestly, judiciously, and sincerely following the above recommended considerations will suffice to tackle the listed problems of India. The pros and cons of following or ignoring this *Happism-based* SOS are given under the sub-title of "PASIE6 Nation" of Part 2 sections "*Happism* Impacts on PASIE Nations" and "PASIE Nations in Absence of *Happism*".

It is easy to say than do. It is true. However, one should employ the philosophy given in Part 2, section "Just Do It". The SOS Format covers all the problems and their solutions in one place at one glance. The "Just Do It" philosophy will help to come up with the blueprint to implement the SOS Format output. If this "*Happism* SOS is not executed properly, the current slippery slope slide will dump the Indian Nation to the center of the "Black Hole." The Indian people at large should remember Principles 2 and 7 when they enter the voting booth. Time is running out before this bad situation gets irreversible.

Illegal Immigration in USA from USA-Mexico Border

A. Problem Definition:

This illegal immigration is a good example of how to solve a national problem using System Orientation Solution (SOS) with built-in 360 degree rationale based on implicit and explicit principles of *Happism* Theory. The current illegal immigration In USA from USA-Mexico border can be divided in the following four categories:

Category 1: Adults illegally entered USA sometimes back. They are the current undocumented workers,

Category 2: Kids brought to USA by their illegally entered adults,

Category 3: Population born out of illegally immigrated parent(s).

Category 4: Continuous flow of illegal immigrants at the pervious USA-Mexico border.

Categories 2 and 3 are causing tremendous strain on economy and education system. High school education is free in USA. This increases student/staff ratio in public schools deteriorating the quality of education. The same situation exists in medical facilities because of the patients from the above four categories. It is needless to describe here all the ills caused by the illegal immigration. One special problem worth mentioning is a rapid growth of Category 3 driven by the unusually high birth rate among Catholic Hispanics in Categories 1 and 4, resulting in a demographic imbalance of USA.

The Catch-22 is: USA needs some of the Categories 1 and 4 personnel for manual work at farm lands, housing, restaurants, environmental and infrastructure projects, etc. Some religious leaders, to increase the number in their congregations, like this illegal immigration of Categories 1 and 4. Politics also plays a major role here, since majority of the Hispanic voters tend to vote democratic. As such, the Democrats and the Republicans do not see eye to eye for any solution to this illegal immigration problem. This has created a political paralysis at the federal and the state levels.

The aim of the current System Oriented Solution (SOS) is to solve this problem on a permanent and sustainable basis with zero consideration to political correctness. For a long time, we have been goofing around the temporary solutions, hog-wash, and beating around the bushes. This will never solve the original problem but will cause progressive deterioration of economy and demography of the nation. The permanent SOS intends to achieve a delicate balance between crime and punishment (Principle 6) and also between economy and obligation (Part 1, section on Social Obligations). In fact, this problem of illegal immigration traps USA- Conscious in a cage of morality and national interest. SOS will liberate it by using both ethical and rational principles of *Happism*.

In light of this situation and also with regards to the Border Consideration of *Happism* Manifesto, implementation of SOS starts with sealing of USA-Mexico border to stop the flow of illegal immigration. Major obstruction put forward to this is high cost of fence or wall necessary to seal the border. I don't believe in this cost excuse when we can waste billions of dollars on unwarranted wars and planning to send a man to Mars. The whole thing begins at "Wall Project" similar to "Manhattan Project", by soliciting the fence/wall ideas from the big brains of our renowned universities and research institutes, then calling Wall Project conference(s) to discuss these ideas. One comprehensive cumulative brilliant idea should be agreed upon enveloping all these bright high-tech gimmicks to start the construction of the wall/fence within the next couple of years or so. Think of the Great Wall of China! They could do it with their primitive technology!! We can surely do it at amazing speed, provided we have a will to do so. Economy is a bogus excuse. Money spent will be recovered in a due course of time.

By definition of "Downtrodden" stated in Part 1, section "Social Obligations towards Forgotten and Downtrodden", Categories 2 and 3 are of Downtrodden. They should be helped by rest of the population because of the moral obligations explained in that section. Therefore, *Happism* Theory recommends legal immigration status of Green Card Holder (GCH) to Categories 2 and 3 who may subsequently apply for citizenship in a due course of time. These Categories are basically assimilated in the boiling pot of USA and will not have unusually high birth rate observed in Categories 1 and 4.

Problems of Categories 1 and 4 will be solved in the following SOS Format. In fact, once the Wall Project is complete, Category 4 will not exist at all.

B. SOS Based on *Happism* Considerations:

Problem of Category 1 illegal immigration from Mexico and Latin America is solved here on a permanent basis employing economic, moral, ethical and practical aspects of HAPPISM Considerations. As mentioned earlier, appropriate balance between crime and punishment will be maintained using the following SOS Format.

1. Population Consideration: WF1 not equal to 0

Compared to the overall population of USA, population of illegal immigrants Category 1 is much smaller. For them, two special immigration categories are recommended here: Blue Card Immigrant (BCI) and Blue Card Citizen (BCC). BCI can apply for BCC status after five years. All the Category 1 illegal immigrants will be given the status of BCI, subjected to the conditions outlined here in various *Happism* Considerations. The Population Consideration demands that BCI person should not have any more kids, if he/she has already two or more. The fine per violation will be $50,000. If the person cannot pay the fine, some deterring jail term will be imposed. Adopting humanitarian approach, deportation is not recommended to avoid separation of family members.

2. Border Consideration: WF2 not equal to 0

Successful execution of Wall Project is a precursor to start implementation of this SOS. There is absolutely no other way about it. I cannot believe: A country economically and scientifically so powerful cannot seal its border. It is "Penny wise, pound foolish" to show economic reason for not doing so. Once the Wall Project is complete, expenses of 20,000 or so border security guards will be drastically reduced. Time will prove it. The reason mentioned in Catch-22 above will be given a proper weightage ahead in Production Consideration of the manifesto. Sealing of the border will make Category 4 nonexistent.

3. Weapon consideration: WF3 not equal to 0

If Category 1 person is found in violation of the weapon laws or has committed any crime at the time of receiving his/her BCI status, then that person will be deported, provided he/she has no family (parents, spouse or children). Remaining BCI violators will be asked to pay special fines depending on the nature of violation (Principle 6). Amount of fine will be decided as follows:

Nonviolent Crime(s): First $10,000; second $25,000; etc.

Violent Crime(s): First $20,000, second $45,000; etc.

Above dollar values are just for example. They may be revised by more knowledgeable personnel. If the violator cannot pay the fine, some jail term will be imposed before giving BCI status. No deportation is recommended for the humanitarian reason mentioned earlier.

4. Science and Technology Research Consideration: WF4 not equal to 0

Categories 2 and 3 should be encouraged to pursue proper education. BCI should be left for basic manual labor for which he/she has entered USA illegally. However, BCI will be encouraged to register for Basic English Language course(s).

5. Production Consideration: WF5 not equal to 0

As mentioned earlier, USA needs some external labor force. This source will be dried when borders are sealed as required by Border Consideration. SOS recommends a new visa category of Voucher Card Holder (VCH). Accordingly, a four years voucher will be issued to proper Mexican and Latin American (Hispanic) people to enter USA and work here in a labor force. VCH will not be allowed to marry or have kids in USA. Violators will have a choice of paying $50,000 fine per violation or will be deported. Based on the demand and supply of the labor force, appropriate number of vouchers will be issued each year. VCH will have to leave USA after four years.

BCI, BCC and VCH personnel may opt for driver's licenses. BCI and VCH are not eligible for food stamps, Medicare, Medicaid or Social Security benefits, whereas, BCC can apply for them after age 62 years. No attempt will be made to recover back taxes at the time of issuing BCI, since that attempt will be like digging in a gold mine where excavation cost is more than the resulting gold revenue. BCI, BCC and VCH card holders will pay the taxes at the same rate as of US citizens.

6. Religious Consideration: WF6 not equal to 0

All the four categories of illegal immigrants should follow the religious philosophy of "Success and Happiness through Virtues" (Principle 13). BCI and BCC should strictly adhere to the policy of number of children per person outlined in Population Consideration above, irrespective of his/her religious belief.

7. Environmental Consideration: WF7 not equal to 0

Environmental work also needs manual labor which will be supplied by VCH category.

C. Discussion of Ideal Solution and Nonideal Eventualities:

Here is the summary of above System Oriented Solution:

(i) First and foremost thing is to execute Wall Project successfully to make USA-Mexico border impervious to illegal immigration.

(ii) Illegal immigrants of Categories 2 and 3 will be given full amnesty without any restriction and be given Green Card and subsequent citizenship, since they are "Downtrodden".

(iii) Illegal immigrants of Category 1 will be issued BCI status and then BCC status with due restrictions imposed in above *Happism* Considerations.

(iv) Manual labor requirements in USA will be fulfilled by the system of VCH explained in Production Consideration above.

(v) Category 4 of illegal immigrants will not exist with the completion of Wall Project.

Once all the fines/punishments are standardized for the various noncompliances of *Happism* Considerations, this System Oriented Solution implementation will itself be System Oriented with minimum bureaucratic interference. Border security guards and other expenses will be drastically reduced. Activities of narcotic dealers and gun runners will be almost nonexistent. Political bickering at state, federal, ethnic and party levels will be considerably less, channeling the efforts to more urgent and useful national, state level, and social agendas.

The notion that the cross-border illegal immigration will die-down automatically, without the presence of the wall or the fence, is a myth. Illegal immigration increases with the improvement of job situation in USA. The irony is: The number of undocumented workers does not go down when US economy is in tail-spin.

It is further noted that this SOS is permanent and sustainable, based on humane and 360 degree rationale of *Happism* Principles. Other current attempts to solve this illegal immigration problem are Half-Baked Potatoes being used as Flying Missiles by various political and ethnic factions. It is essential to execute this SOS at earliest before the economic and the demographic situation in USA goes from bad to worse to irreversible.

Human Beings: Fish Type 4?

Is the human race like Fish Type 4; which commits the same mistakes again and again and stays sickly forever? We, the human beings, proudly proclaim the difference between us and other primates: The latter don't have the means to communicate the knowledge from generation to generation; as a result every generation rediscovers the same thing again and again. Human beings do have these means, and yet many of us repeat the same age-old mistakes!!—Are we dumber than other primates? I am not here to describe a grim landscape of humanity. However, I see many people, rich and poor alike, bobbing up and down in a vast ocean of uncertainties and worries. Also, I see a few tiny islands of *happiness* that are under a constant threat of flooding due to *global warming* and frequent waves of *economic uncertainties*. Well, we get what we deserve! God has given us a brilliant brain, but if we misuse it to execute wrong notions of *success* and *happiness*, then we are the only one to be blamed. We should never forget that aim of personal success is creation and spread of happiness. Many miseries we individually face are the direct offshoots of our violations of the fundamental principles and philosophies given in Part 1 during the discourse on *success* and *happiness*.

Apart from the forces from the fifth dimension, most of our national and international problems are our own creations. The story of the Four Fish is of special significance here, but unfortunately, the human race is of Fish Type 4: Old problems are unsolved and the similar new ones pop up again and again on the world scene. The tragedy is, we try to solve them with wrong philosophies and selfish intentions. To avoid recurrences of the same problem, System Oriented Solution (SOS) of Part 3 is best suited, since it is evolved from the unbiased, ethical, 360 degrees rationale based on *Happism* Theory.

We should remember here that SOS is for a given national or international problem and not for creating permanent and sustainable happiness on Planet Earth. That can be achieved only by the complete execution of the *Happism* Manifesto of Part 2. Therefore, I again urge the world powers and superpowers to exert their influence in UNO and make the world nations follow the *Happism* Manifesto in earnest. Without this implementation of *Happism* Manifesto, we the human beings will never attain the happiness level god has intended by giving us a brilliant brain and the beautiful Mother Earth. However, no matter what happiness level we attain, life will go on till the sun shines and the Earth stays in its orbit. The question is: What type of world will we leave behind for our future generations?

APPENDIX 1
Implementation of "Happism" Based System Oriented Solution (SOS) of Palestine Problem

"Happism" Theory and its Manifesto are given in Part 2 of this book. The theory aims at permanent and sustainable happiness on Planet Earth. It is not some abstract or Utopian theory, since it has a direct application in the form of System Oriented Solution (SOS) to solve national and international problems, such as Illegal Immigration in USA, Global Warming, Gun Homicide Rate in USA, etc. This SOS, as applied to Palestine Problem, is incorporated in Part 3 under subtitle Palestine Problem.

As a first glance at the proposed SOS, the latter may appear simplistic. But it is to be noted that the solution is "Ideal". All the comprehensive attempts to solve Palestine Problem should aim at achieving this final "Ideal" state of Palestine. Currently, some desperate attempts are being made to solve this problem. These attempts are something like extinguishing a local brush fire, leaving the original blaze burning with full vicious vigor. On the contrary, SOS given in Part 3 is permanent and sustainable, so long as it is followed judiciously.

SOS of Palestine Problem of Part 3 is to be executed in the following manner to achieve the "Ideal" situation. This step-by-step execution is given here in the following Sections A, B, and C with due considerations to the fundamentals of "Happism" Principles derived in Part 3 and cited here as used basis.

SOS Execution of Palestine Problem

A. Background of Palestine Problem:

Considering the complex nature, the implementation of SOS is carried-out step-by-step. The first thing to be considered is Part 3 Principle 9:

Principle 9: - - - Through the humanitarian point of view, it is the bounden duty of world nations to actively intervene in a domestic conflict of any nation to end the large scale massacre of its innocent civilians, if the massacre is resulting from that domestic conflict. Palestine problem has created a mass scale suffering of people for generations together, so much so that it has become a big blot on entire humanity. Palestinians cannot execute SOS themselves alone. It is the moral duty of the rest of the world to help them, as postulated in Principle 9. Once the problem is solved, Palestinians themselves will be responsible not to recreate it and maintain the situation implied in the "Ideal" solution prescribed in SOS of Sections A, B, and C of Part 3. Considering the current state of affair, Palestinians and the rest of the world nations should adopt the following procedure to implement the above "Ideal" SOS.

B. Implementation of SOS:

1. Population Consideration: At the initial stage of implementation, this factor is of less consequence. But after the SOS is completely executed, Palestinians should give due consideration to maintain their population at a sustainable level in par with the available resources. Reduction in population density, particularly in Gaza Strip, should be given high priority.

2. Border Consideration: The Palestine State, as defined by UNO Resolution, should secure its borders against the flow of unauthorized weapons and the influx of illegal immigrants, who are basically the terrorists. Also, the existing illegals should be deported or removed by force. As it is obvious, Palestinians alone are not capable of achieving such ideal situation. Rest of the world nations should help them in this endeavor. However, Israel will be, for most of the operation, a passive observer since its active involvement will again add fuel to the fire. The current trading routes of Gaza Strip blocked by Egypt and Israel should be opened with due safeguards against their misuse by the Palestinians, who will be ultimately responsible for the consequences of any misuse. Israeli settlements built in Palestine

State should be handed over to Palestine, after a due compensation.

3.   Weapon Consideration: This consideration is for the establishment of terrorists-free internal law and order and also to safeguard against external aggression. Once the borders are secured and the terrorists are flushed out or eliminated with the help of other nations, arming of the Palestinians should be undertaken. This necessitates a delicate balance between the two apparently opposing conditions: (a) Palestine should have adequate National Security Forces (NSF) and the weapons to seal the borders, also to stem mushrooming of anti-Israel elements; (b) The Israel nation should have an absolute guarantee that the Palestinians have no sophisticated weapons to attack Israel. The solution for this catch-22 situation is NSF should be armed as a paramilitary force without any war related weapons such as tanks, artilleries, missiles, bombs, automatic weapons, etc. After the complete execution of above catch-22 solution and SOS of Sections A, B, and C of Part 3, if miscreants in Palestine continue to play mischief against Israel, then the Palestinians will be fully responsible for the subsequent consequences. They should remember Part 3 Principle 14: Unhappy are those who deserve to be unhappy, barring the forces from the fifth dimension (forces beyond one's control).

4. Science and Technology Research Consideration: The Palestinians should give a special emphasis on science, technology and general education of their masses. The world nations should help the Palestinians during this endeavor.

5. Production Consideration: Palestine State should satisfy its daily needs and defense requirements by maintaining the adequate production level. Generous help from other nations is expected during this formative period of Palestine State.

6. Religious Consideration: The Palestinians should implement the recommendations of SOS of Part 3 under Religious Consideration.

7. Environmental Consideration: No execution of this SOS Consideration is needed at the initial stage.

C. Discussion of Implementation Procedure:

The idea behind this implementation procedure of SOS is to urge rest of the world nations to help Palestinians to secure borders and to get rid of the miscreants and their missiles, tunnel network, etc. Also, the Palestinian refugees should be given full citizenships of the countries they have been living in prior to Syrian War. When these conditions are satisfied and the Palestinians themselves are able enough to maintain the impervious borders and terrorists-free internal law and order, the armies of other nations can be pulled out handing over the tasks to Palestinians. However, other nations should continue to help Palestine economically also through technical know-how to sustain it as a viable nation. Remaining is the responsibility of the Palestinians to prove their worth as a member of world nations. That will grant Palestine a voting right as a full-fledged member of UNO.

The SOS of Part 3 with its implementation procedure outlined in this Appendix is the only chance to bring permanent and sustainable peace and tranquility to Palestine State and much extent to Israel also.